Collecting

American

Decorative Arts

and Sculpture

◆ ◆ ◆

1971-1991

Collecting American Decorative Arts and Sculpture

◆ ◆ ◆

1971-1991

INTRODUCTION
Jonathan L. Fairbanks

CONTRIBUTORS
Edward S. Cooke, Jr., Jeannine J. Falino,
Linda L. Foss, Rachel J. Monfredo,
Maria Pulsone

Museum of Fine Arts
Boston

CONTENTS

FOREWORD

This exhibition and catalogue celebrate the 20th anniversary of the founding of the Department of American Decorative Arts and Sculpture at the Museum of Fine Arts, Boston. The Museum has been actively collecting American decorative arts and sculpture since as early as 1877, pioneering the systematic collecting of American silver in the early years of this century and acquiring by gift the marvelous M. & M. Karolik collection of American furniture of the Colonial and Early Federal periods between 1939 and 1941. The founding of the department twenty years ago was a reaffirmation of the Museum's commitment to the decorative arts and sculpture of America, and subsequent departmental activity has been extraordinarily dynamic. Generous gifts have enabled the collection to grow in depth as well as in breadth, and have strengthened the larger scholarly mission of the department through support of research, publications, and exhibitions of the highest quality. This exhibition presents a concentrated survey of the recent collecting activity of the department, celebrating the achievements of the past and hinting at new and innovative directions for the future.

ALAN SHESTACK
Director

ACKNOWLEDGMENTS

This exhibition and catalogue, which celebrate the twentieth anniversary of the founding of the Department of American Decorative Arts and Sculpture, would not have been possible without the assistance and help of many friends and colleagues. We are most grateful for the constant and generous support of the members of the Department's Visiting Committee and the Seminarians, a collectors' study group associated with the department. The Wunsch Foundation provided funding for the publication of the catalogue. Present and past members of the department (listed at the end of the book) have contributed considerable expertise and energies in building, maintaining, and interpreting the collection. For specific information concerning objects in the catalogue, we would like to acknowledge several colleagues in particular: David Barquist, Frank Coolidge, Ulysses G. Dietz, Rosemary Joyce, Patricia E. Kane, Walter J. Karcheski, Jr., Susan Montgomery, David Rago, Thomas Siegel, Charles Venable, Catherine Hoover Voorsanger, Barbara Ward, Deborah Dependahl Waters, Gregory Weidman, Roger Wilson, and James Yarnell. The consummate upholstery work on nearly all the furniture, and our own understanding of that art and craft, was provided by the Museum's upholstery consultant, Andrew Passeri. For the treatment of the Baltimore Grecian couch, we would like to express our appreciation to Elizabeth Lahikainen and the staff of the Conservation Lab at the Society for the Preservation of New England Antiquities.

Within the Museum of Fine Arts, we would like to thank Janice Sorkow, Director of Photographic Services for patiently overseeing the extensive photography, and Tom Lang, John Lutsch, Gary Ruuska, Marty Wolfand, and John Woolf for their sensitive photographs. Judith Downes and Susan Wong of the Design Department fit the large number of objects into a confined space with a grace that permits individual inspection and overall sense of accomplishment. Gilian Wohlauer of the Department of Education helped to write the exhibition labels. In the preparation of the catalog, Cynthia Purvis carefully read through the manuscript with insight and provided great clarity to the project. Cynthia Randall molded the written and pictorial parts into a graphically pleasing whole. In our furniture conservation lab, Robert Walker, Susan Walker, and Letitia Stevens worked long and hard to prepare the furniture for photography and exhibition. Their input was also essential in the development of new scholarly analysis. We would also like to thank Theodore E. Stebbins, Jr., John Moors Cabot Curator of American Painting, and the staff of the Department of Paintings for their willingness to include in the exhibition several American paintings that have been acquired through the efforts of the Department of American Decorative Arts and Sculpture.

The catalogue is dedicated to the memory of former staff members:

Mary C. Quinn (1949-1984)
Joyce Goldberg (1950-1987)
Laurie W. Crichton (1953-1979)
Kathryn C. Buhler (1901-1986)

INTRODUCTION

Jonathan L. Fairbanks
Katharine Lane Weems Curator of
American Decorative Arts and Sculpture

Visitors are sometimes puzzled by the rough, uncarved stone in the pediment over the Museum's Huntington Avenue doorway. Was the block left uncarved because of financial constraints, or was it left unfinished in order to remind the viewer that a museum's work is never complete? These questions address fundamental institutional concerns. Museums cannot flourish without perpetual funding, and of course, the work of collecting, care, and interpretation is never complete. While the financial constraints of museums are well understood, the dynamic nature of a collection seems less so. From time to time people claim that collecting is becoming an obsolete function of art museums. Yet this reflects a viewpoint of personal rather than public collecting. To meet or challenge the needs and expectations of every succeeding generation, museums need to continually develop. Like libraries, museums must continue to make significant additions. Otherwise they become fossils of past taste. Just as new understanding about art comes through new discoveries and new acquisitions, so also public enjoyment is dependent on collection vitality.

How or why a work of art is singled out for a museum collection may be an utter mystery to the average visitor. This catalogue attempts to shed some light by exploring the growth and development of collections of three-dimensional arts of America at the MFA. The works in this exhibition are selected from more than 2,800 objects collected since the Department of American Decorative Arts and Sculpture was founded twenty years ago. Works range in date from the present day to prehistoric America and span the entire continent, representing the ethnic panorama of American art history. Such a small sampler cannot be comprehensive, but it does show how the Museum's collections have stretched into unexplored time frames and cultural strands. At the same time the Museum has added significant depth to the early New England holdings that were here before 1971.

How this came about requires a review of contributions made by extraordinarily generous donors, contributing supporters, and the insightful, energetic curatorial staff. Visitors who take the trouble to read credit lines on labels will discover that a high percentage of objects acquired came as gifts, with little or no direct cost to the Museum or its endowment. Such giving represents a dynamic public commitment. However the art thus collected honors not only donors but also staff members, who use their abilities and insights to search for important objects. It is a constant adventure to discover, among thousands of available works of art, significant patterns, qualities, and meanings that represent the best or most compelling statements from America's past and present. Once discovered and acquired, the object engages conservation, research, and publication as well as public display. Collections grow in many different ways and each way represents different aspects of human personality, individual memory, taste, attitude, skill and patronage that, bundled together, help explain the variegated culture of America. These activities make collecting a compelling quest, and keep museums alive and responsive to human needs.

The Department of American Decorative Arts and Sculpture was established by vote of the Board of Trustees in January of 1970, the Museum's centennial year. As the director, Perry T. Rathbone, stated in the Museum's annual report of 1969-1970, "The Museum's collections in this field are extensive and varied, and the responsibility of maintaining them, enriching them, and interpreting them has become too great to be discharged properly without full curatorial specialization and commitment." Until this point there had only been assistant curators who worked with American material in a department that included both European and American decorative arts and sculpture. Despite the considerable reputation that the MFA collection enjoyed in the American field, it was losing ground in a rapidly expanding and changing discipline. Since the 1950s, increased public and scholarly interest in American decorative arts had been reflected in new collecting philosophies, and museums were seeking to increase their collections. At the MFA the American design arts after 1825 were underrepresented. Many collectors of the older generation believed that mechanization had eroded the artistic quality in the arts produced after that date. Richard Randall, who served as assistant curator before leaving in 1964 to become the assistant director of the Walters

Art Gallery in Baltimore, had broken through this prejudice by collecting a few superb examples of furniture designed by the great Boston architect, Henry Hobson Richardson, but these acquisitions proved the exception. Collecting American Victorian arts was discouraged even though the Museum already owned several exceptional stained glass windows designed by John La Farge. It was also almost unthinkable to collect early twentieth-century or contemporary decorative arts. For want of direct support or advocacy for the American arts, the MFA was failing to keep pace with new collecting possibilities. Even the seventeenth-and eighteenth-century period rooms on the court floor were neglected. They became shabby and were closed to public view.

Despite this period of quiescence at the MFA, two staff members did their best to enhance the American decorative arts after Randall's departure. The leading scholar in historic American silver, Kathryn C. Buhler, who had worked at the Museum since the 1920s, was completing the manuscript for a superb two-volume catalogue of American silver owned by the MFA. In 1968, with the help of Mrs. J. Wallace McMeel, Mrs. Antony Edger, and Mrs. C. Vincent Vappi, assistant curator Henry H. Schnabel, Jr., and others established a study group of young collectors in an effort to develop and nurture local interest in Americana and to build support for the American collections at the MFA. The group met monthly in seminar fashion and called themselves The Seminarians.

In 1969, the Ladies Committee mounted a successful public auction of donated antiques and earmarked the proceeds for the exclusive use of the new department. This enabled Perry Rathbone to invite me to serve as the Museum's first full curator in American arts. The opportunity to develop a new department within one of America's greatest museums proved irresistible, and I accepted the appointment as of 1 January 1971, to begin full-time work in Boston in June.[1]

During the transition the first assistant, Gilian Wohlauer, organized the office and I initiated a furniture conservation laboratory at the MFA. Much of the furniture was in deplorable condition so I sought the services of Vincent Cerbone, a highly skilled cabinetmaker trained in Italy whose talents were under-utilized in the Museum's carpentry shop.[2] To this day, the furniture conservation laboratory, whose staff and resources are shared with the European Decorative Arts and Sculpture Department, is a vital part of the Museum collections program.

Just as the furniture conservation laboratory was organized before I arrived full-time, so also collecting began. A handsome silver teapot (exh. no. 34) made by Zachariah Brigden (1734-1787) of Boston, which had been on loan from a private owner from 1950 to 1970, was withdrawn and placed at auction. When no bid surpassed the reserve (a price below which the work would not be sold), the director and the Collections Committee acquired it through the Theodora Wilbour Fund in Memory of Charlotte Beebe Wilbour in early 1971. The teapot added an important note of taste from a family that commissioned engravings by Paul Revere and paintings by John Singleton Copley. Hence the first acquisition for the new department built upon collection strengths rather than signalling a new departure.

The same could be said of an even more magnificent object given later that year: a teakettle and stand (52*) by Jacob Hurd (1702-1758) of Boston engraved with the Lowell family arms impaled by Leveredge. The robust form, effusive cast ornament, and sure engraving make this tea kettle and stand among the finest of its type by one of the greatest goldsmiths of mid-eighteenth century America. It was given by a descendent of the Lowells through Esther Lowell Abbott in memory of her mother, Esther Lowell Cunningham, granddaughter of James Russell Lowell, the writer. As interesting as this pedigree is, an untutored visitor might ask what benefit such detail offers the viewer. One answer is that museums are keepers of memory as well as works of art. The provenance and historical associations of an object help to reveal its meaning, and form the basis of future scholarship. A work of art cut off from its provenance is a fragment that cries for reconstruction. Serious collectors, fully aware of the value of associated historical data, collect as much information as possible at the time of acquisition.

*Bold numbers refer to illustrations

Serious collecting is a creative pursuit attempted by many but successfully achieved by only a few. At my first meeting with the Seminarians I had the good fortune to visit with Boston's greatest collector of early American furniture. Edward C. Johnson III is private about his collection, and so I knew nothing about its size or quality. In September 1971, Johnson was elected to the Board of Trustees of the Museum and became the chairman of the department's Visiting Committee.[3] Johnson's election was a turning point for the new department: he understood the necessity of improving collections, broadening their scope, and developing their national character. With his encouragement, I instituted a new collecting philosophy that included categories of objects rarely or never collected in the past. Although I began to seek mid-to late-nineteenth-century works of art, twentieth-century objects, and Native American arts, the actual acquisition process was gradual.

As important as the enterprise of staff and the advice of friends was, so also were donations from unexpected quarters. For example, Mrs. George P. Montgomery of New York had kept a silver teapot by Paul Revere, Sr., in a bank vault for years. As work by Paul Revere, Sr., was even more scarce than that by his more famous son, Mrs. Montgomery was fearful of keeping it in her home. A friend advised her to donate it to the Museum and suggested that I contact her. The simple, round teapot (1972.122) was a welcome addition to the Museum's extensive holdings of Revere family works. Kathryn C. Buhler, who remained active in the department as a fellow for research, persuaded two friends in Cambridge — Miss Martha May Eliot and Miss Abigail Adams Eliot — to donate a handsome silver tea set (exh. no. 50) made by Charles Boehme of Baltimore, about 1800. This was the first Baltimore silver to enter the Museum's collections.

Within a year another piece of Baltimore silver, a splendid ceremonial sword (exh. no. 50), made about 1825 by Thomas and Andrew Ellicott Warner, was offered by a dealer. The funds were donated by William N. Banks, an important collector of the arts of classical America and a member of the department's Visiting Committee. The sword initiated interest in the mature classical revival in America. Banks provided the leadership and means for many important acquisitions in the American arts of the early National period, including a pair of gilded New York pier tables (exh. no. 48), a pair of Boston pier tables bearing the label of the Boston makers George Archibald and Thomas Emmons (1972.652, 653), and a Boston-made cellarette (1978.125). This collection of masterworks dating between 1813 and 1824 has attracted significant gifts from other individuals of classical-style American furniture and silver to the Museum, including a Salem center table (exh. no. 52) and a secretaire à abattant (1985.335) labeled by Archibald and Emmons. Perhaps the most dramatic recent example was a Grecian couch (15) made in Baltimore, whose purchase was made possible by the support of several members of the Visiting Committee and the Edward J. Holmes Fund. This exhibition marks the first time that couch has been displayed or published since its purchase.

An unusual gift was arranged in late 1971 by the late David Stockman, a former development officer for Boston College who was a generous friend to the department. He learned that a large collection of pottery and glass assembled by Professor Emeritus Frederick H. Norton had been left at MIT after Professor Norton's retirement from the Department of Metallurgy and Material Science. With the permission of Norton and his former department, the vast majority of the collection of 194 objects came as a gift to the Museum (1971.442-616 and .651-.671). I originally thought that the collection was a wonderful teaching and study resource and that the whole was more significant than the individual parts. We later discovered that the collection included several individual masterworks, including the "intarsia" vase (70) by Frederick Carder, chief designer of the Steuben Glass Works. This example highlights the importance of collecting broadly; had I selected only the few pieces that caught my eye, this important vase would likely have been overlooked.

As the Department gained momentum in the early 1970s, the staff, which consisted of a secretary, assistant curator, and curatorial assistant, was augmented with work-study graduate students from Boston University's American and New England Studies Program. Volunteers and interns played important roles in the various activities of exhibitions and collections. The furniture conservation laboratory gained the exceptional talent of Robert Walker, an English-trained cabinetmaker who is now in charge of furniture conservation. With such personnel it was possible to mount three small exhibitions to investigate aspects of seventeenth-, eighteenth- and nineteenth-century American arts. The first of these, "Plymouth Re-Collected," was held in 1971 and featured works loaned by Pilgrim Hall in Plymouth, Massachusetts. This exhibition exposed staff and visitors to some of the earliest furniture and decorative art objects of New England.

In March 1972, a second exhibition contrasted furniture designed by Boston architect Henry Hobson Richardson with that designed by his Philadelphia contemporary, Frank Furness. This exhibition, the first museum display of Furness-designed furniture, coincided with the initial meeting of the New England chapter of the Victorian Society in America. With the exhibition signalling an interest in Victorian arts, the Museum began vigorously collecting American decorative arts made between 1830 and 1900.

A third exhibition — this one focusing on eighteenth-century Boston furniture — opened in May of 1972, accompanied by a small catalogue and checklist. In conjunction with the show a two-day scholarly conference on eighteenth-century Boston furniture was sponsored by the Colonial Society of Massachusetts. Papers from that conference were published as a book with the editorial assistance of Brock Jobe, a recent Winterthur fellow and Boston University doctoral candidate who joined the Department under a grant from the National Endowment for the Arts.[4]

Perhaps due to the conference or perhaps by mere coincidence, the 1972-1973 fiscal year was a banner one for collecting mainstream Boston silver and furniture. Even as Katherine Buhler's superb catalogue of the Museum's American silver collection was off the press and being honored by an exhibition: "Art and Mystery: American Silver, 1655-1825," the Museum purchased a very important piece of American silver. A silver punch bowl (50) by Boston's greatest early eighteenth-century goldsmith, John Coney (1655/6-1722), had been discovered in England the year before. It was the first major piece of silver made in America to express the Georgian style. An earlier piece by Coney, a chocolate pot (51) joined the collection permanently after fifty-two years of loan through a generous partial gift and partial sale to the Museum by its owner, Dr. Lamar Soutter.

Another colonial Boston masterpiece — a bombé chest-on-chest (9) signed by its maker, John Cogswell of Boston, and dated 1782 — was acquired directly from descendants of Elias Hasket Derby, for whom the work was originally made. Pictured in color on the cover of the 1971-72 annual report, it was the most important piece of American furniture to be purchased by any museum in many years. While it is not possible, without revealing confidences, to identify all those who helped with the complexities of this acquisition, they know they made it possible for this great piece of Boston furniture to come to the Museum rather than to migrate out of the state.

Also in 1972 Richard Edwards of Peru, Indiana, informed us of his willingness to donate more than 200 objects that family tradition held were originally from the Derby/West family home known as Oak Hill. The woodwork of three rooms from this building, which once stood near Peabody, Massachusetts, was already installed at the Museum. Edwards's generous gift provided a unique opportunity to refurnish the rooms, which had not received much curatorial attention since they were first installed in the late 1920s. Superb examples of Federal New England architecture, the rooms were shabby after many years of neglect, and the upholstered furniture was too worn to display.

I closed the rooms in 1975 for research and reinstallation, confident that the Edwards gift would guarantee a prompt reopening. Assistant curator Anne Farnam, a former Boston University intern, began the research. During the following eight years of research and reinstallation, several other members of the curatorial staff successively headed the project. The rooms were finally opened, refurnished and completely renewed, in 1983.[5] In the process I learned a basic lesson of museum work: once closed, museum rooms or galleries become convenient storage space that makes reopening almost impossible. Without the deadline imposed by a grant from the National Endowment for the Arts the rooms might still be closed.

During the 1972 Christmas holidays Gilian Wohlauer, who had served as the assistant to the curator since the founding of the Department, mounted an exhibition of Santos loaned by the Instituto de Cultura Puertorriquena, San Juan, from the Island of Puerto Rico. The catalogue, *Santos de Puerto Rico*, written in both Spanish and English, illustrated the carved and painted wooden figures made by pious folk artists. As a direct result of this exhibition — the department's first step toward ethnic diversity — Mr. and Mrs. Walter Fillin of New York donated a fine collection of twenty-two Santos from Puerto Rico (1973.250-271), a region never before represented in the collections. By 1973 it was clear that special exhibitions were the most effective way to attract potential donors.

When a space suddenly opened in the 1974 exhibition calendar, I developed an exhibition about American art of the Victorian period drawn from the Museum's permanent collections. Called "Confident America: Monuments in Painting, Sculpture, and Prints," it displayed American materials from a number of departments: textiles, prints, drawings, paintings, furniture, sculpture, and musical instruments. The Museum's rich collection of American marble sculpture of the Victorian era, banished to storage for more than a dozen years, emerged freshly cleaned and staged in a sequence of four galleries that rendered contrasting themes or ideas from the nineteenth century. The renewed interest in American nineteenth-century sculpture led to the purchase of a superb sculpture by Horatio Greenough of his pet greyhound, *Arno* (30). It was acquired from Gerald Horrigan, a guard who was stationed in the exhibition. It had originally been offered to the Museum in the 1920s and refused because early American sculpture had passed out of style. Neither I, the director, nor members of the Museum's Collection Committee repeated the earlier mistake. *Arno* is one of the most popularly admired pieces of neoclassical American sculpture in the Museum.

In 1974, when the Pewter Collectors Club in America held its annual meeting in Boston, the Museum played host and presented a special display of American pewter from the permanent collection. The collection was carefully cleaned by pewter collector William O. Blaney, with the assistance of Nancy Webbe and Eleuthera du Pont. Anne Farnam orchestrated the installation and the production of a superb pictorial catalogue, which was distributed to members of the club. Daniel Farber of Worcester photographed the pewter illustrated in the catalogue and donated both prints and negatives to the Museum.[6] These photographs were described by a leading connoisseur of American art, the late Charles F. Montgomery of Yale University, as the finest photographs of pewter in existence. While the Museum did not acquire any pewter as a result of this exhibition, its pewter was properly cleaned, catalogued and photographed in preparation for the exhibition and catalogue.

Perhaps most importantly the photography of the pewter established a lasting relationship with Dan Farber. As a friend of the department, Dan had already donated several hundred magnificent large-format photographs of New England tombstones. These donations began early in the 1970s and have continued to the present day. They represent a lifetime dedicated to the preservation and pictorial documentation of grave markers as works of art. While most of Dan's photographs are catalogued for study purposes and kept in the Museum's archives, a superb sample hangs in the seventeenth-century corridor galleries, above furniture contemporaneous with the tombstones pictured. In addition to giving time, service and money to assist the department in its collections growth, Dan and his wife, Jessie-Lie (both departmental Visitors), have arranged for a select group of actual stones to come to the Museum on loan in order to preserve them from vandalism and weathering. The most important of these are the head and foot stone of the grave of John Foster, America's first printmaker who is buried in the Dorchester burying ground. Through Dan's efforts, a replica of the stone was made for that site and the proper legal steps were taken to remove it to the Museum.

By 1974 there was no doubt that the department would play a major role in helping the Museum celebrate the American bicentennial. Two scholars, Elizabeth Sussman and Wendy Cooper, were appointed as special assistants to develop, respectively, *Frontier America: The Far West* and *Paul Revere's Boston: 1735-1818*. Grants from the National Endowment for the Arts supported both exhibitions, and a grant from Philip Morris Incorporated, on behalf of Marlboro, ensured that *Frontier America* would travel to several museums across the United States and thereafter, in 1976, abroad to the Hague, Zurich, Essen and Vienna. The two exhibitions could not have been more different. The Far West exhibition focused on the arts of the common man west of the Mississippi River during the nineteenth century and therefore drew talents and collections from across America. The Revere exhibition, on the other hand, featured the most stylish arts of Boston's elite of the eighteenth and early nineteenth centuries, and relied heavily upon the collections of such nearby institutions as the American Antiquarian Society in Worcester and the Massachusetts Historical Society in Boston.[7]

While the Far West exhibition had little promise of attracting objects to the Museum's collection, it did challenge preconceived notions about what was appropriate for an urban art museum to exhibit as legitimate art. It stretched the yardstick of artistic values and laid a strong foundation for more ecumenical collecting. As a result of the Revere exhibition, the Museum acquired a superb double chairback settee of the eighteenth century that had originally been owned by Priscilla Scollay of Boston (exh. no. 33). Ronald Bourgeault, a dealer who has contributed greatly to the development of the Museum's collections, brought the private ownership of the settee to the staff's attention. After the Revere exhibition closed, the settee remained at the Museum until it was acquired in 1977. It is one of the best examples of only a handful of similar settees that have survived from eighteenth-century Boston.

In 1974 while staffmembers were planning these two exhibitions, they were also pushing the collections well into the twentieth century. The New England chapter of the American Institute of Interior Designers had presented the Museum with two pieces of contemporary furniture designed by Edward J. Wormley and made by The Dunbar Company (1974.457,458). Wormley, in turn, made a donation of two chairs designed by his friend, industrial designer Charles Eames. These chairs (22 and 1975.32) were displayed in a 1947 landmark exhibition designed by Ludwig Mies van der Rohe at the Museum of Modern Art.

At the same time that these production prototypes came to the Museum, I obtained a grant from the National Endowment for the Arts (matched with a gift from the Gillette Corporation), to provide gallery seating made by contemporary studio furniture-makers. The first artist asked to make furniture for this "Please Be Seated" program was Sam Maloof of Alta Loma, California. For a relatively modest fee he produced a dozen pieces of furniture (23). The public responded enthusiastically to the reminder that the art of fine furniture making is alive and well in America today. One unexpected benefit of allowing visitors to touch the new studio furniture was a marked decline in vandalism.

Perhaps the most impressive single acquisition of the mid-seventies was a gift of six stained glass panels (71) made between 1877 and 1878 under the direction of John La Farge (1835-1910) for the William Watts Sherman House of Newport, Rhode Island. The house is a seminal work in the career of its architect, Henry Hobson Richardson, and the windows are La Farge's first major essay in glass. The donor, James F. O'Gorman, a university professor well-known for his Richardson scholarship, had the presence of mind to preserve these windows when they were removed during renovations made on the Sherman House many years before. He transported the windows through various moves, and finally decided to place them at the Museum, where an important group of La Farge glass already existed.

Another major donation by scholar-colleagues took place in 1975. In that year a large number of works of art that had been on loan to the Museum from the Boston Athenaeum since the Museum's founding were withdrawn for disposal. Classical schol-

ars and curators Cornelius Vermeule III and Emily Vermeule made a generous donation that kept the most important American marble of the era of the Greek revival at
the Museum: Thomas Crawford's *Orpheus and Cerberus* (31). Cornelius continues to
make important gifts to American sculpture, particularly building an impressive collection of medallic arts.

After the *Orpheus* acquisition the staff continued to discover collecting opportunities
in neoclassical American sculpture. In 1977, Jan M. Seidler joined the staff as an NEA
intern from Boston University's American and New England Studies Program. Her first
task was to compile an inventory of Boston's furniture craftsmen of the nineteenth century in order to extend the department's index of eighteenth-century Boston cabinetmakers. Soon she became the assistant curator and discovered the work of sculptor
William Wetmore Story (1819-1895).[8] His beautiful 1863 marble *Sappho* (32) had just
been acquired from a dealer in Tennessee. While the sculptor himself had considered
this work his most appealing idealization, the Museum's Collections Committee expressed some reluctance about its suitability for purchase: at least one member of the
committee was uncomfortable with its Victorian sentiment. Although the sculpture
passed into the collection, it seemed to do so without much enthusiasm. Such is the
natural consequence of collecting works of an era that has not become fully fashionable. If this sculpture were to become available today, there would be no reluctance to
acquire it, but the price would make it unattainable.

Collecting takes patience as well as conviction. Such was the case with a soft-paste
porcelain fruit basket (37) I discovered in 1965 in the home of the late Dr. Horace G.
Richards, a friend with whom I had worked at the Academy of Natural Sciences, Philadelphia, in the mid-1950s. When I found the basket in his china cupboard, I explained
to him and to his sister, Marie, that their family heirloom was one of the greatest rari-
ties of America's earliest porcelain. The American China Manufactory had only oper-
ated a factory between 1770 and 1772, when the business went bankrupt. A mere
handful of works from this firm survive. The Richards were surprised, for a similar
piece was also owned by another relative. That second piece was quickly acquired by
Graham Hood, then curator at the Detroit Institute of Arts. A dozen years later, the
Richards family decided to part with its treasure, which became an important addition
to the Museum's collection.

Timing has much to do with both collecting and exhibiting works of art. The American bicentennial helped to excite a broader public about American arts. In addition to
the special exhibitions the department mounted, we decided to begin exhibiting American sculpture, which in the 1950s had been banished to the basement storage. To this
core collection we added in 1977 a splendid small bronze *Head of Victory* (33) by Augustus Saint-Gaudens (1848-1907). Soon thereafter the Museum acquired a life size
bronze figure of *Young Diana* (1979.121) by Anna Hyatt Huntington (1876-1973).
These, and other finds, led to a 1979 exhibition about women and sculpture. Timely
and thematically coherent, "The Sublime and the Beautiful: Images of Women in
American Sculpture, 1840-1930" was handsomely installed in the Tapestry Gallery
and accompanied by a small but perceptively written catalogue by Jan Seidler and
Kathryn Greenthal. The catalogue featured two new accessions on its first illustration
and back cover — an 1863 marble, *Pandora* (1979.200) by Chauncey B. Ives and a
life-size marble *Nydia, The Blind Girl of Pompeii* (1973.617) made by Randolph Rogers in Rome in 1856. This marble was found in a greenhouse known as Treeland, on
Memorial Drive, Cambridge. It was slowly eroding through exposure to moisture, and
moss grew around the base. Its gift by Dr. and Mrs. Lawrence Perchick was an act of
preservation as well as public patrimony; it has been much appreciated by Museum
visitors in the Victorian American galleries. Rogers's sculpture has not always been so
admired. His family willed the entire contents of his studio to the University of Michigan many years ago. Through neglect hardly a trace of that gift survives. Because
changing tastes do have a real impact on the preservation or demise of works of art, it
is an important task of the curator to rescue works from obscurity and neglect.

In 1978, the Museum also received a gift of approximately 650 pieces of American glass from Mrs. William H. Fenn III (68). The bulk of the collection consisted of blown glassware from the first half of the nineteenth century, including examples from South Boston, Sandwich, New Hampshire, Ohio, and Pittsburgh glass factories. The quality and variety of the collection renewed staff interest in American glass. Soon after the Fenn gift a major collection of pieces of Sandwich pressed glass was donated by department Visitor Kenneth Wakefield and his daughter, Mary Jane. The Wakefield collection (exh. no. 61), which had been on loan and on view in the Museum before the department was formed, was given in memory of Ruth Wakefield, former Visitor and member of the Ladies Committee, who was a vital help to the department in its formative years. With intensified interest in glass, staff began to make excellent use of the Dorothy-Lee Jones Fund to acquire examples of American glass not represented in the Museum (exh. no. 54). American glass collecting continues as illustrated by the gift of fifteen historical flasks given by Mrs. Philip B. Holmes in honor of former Museum president George Seybolt.

As collecting entails care, the curatorial and furniture conservation staff worked together to fill a serious gap in knowledge of period upholstery methods and materials. Andrew Passeri, a master upholsterer with more than fifty years experience, collaborated with curators and conservators, analyzing tacking patterns, old foundations, and fiber fragments to reconstruct the original appearances of much historic upholstery. While his work with Robert Trent, a research associate and chief organizer of the 1982 exhibition "New England Begins: The Seventeenth Century," was particularly important, it is no exaggeration to say that every well-upholstered historic piece of furniture in the Museum has benefited from Andrew's skills and his devotion to his art.

In 1978 the staff began collaborating with Jane C. Nylander, then curator of textiles at Old Sturbridge Village, to develop a conference on historic upholstery in order to accurately represent historic furniture, window hangings, and related design matters. Under the aegis of the Decorative Arts Society and with a grant from the National Endowment for the Arts, scholars came from across the country and abroad to deliver papers, share experiences, and express needs and opportunities. The conference stimulated scholarly interchange and served as a major catalyst for the establishment of the field of upholstery conservation. A lasting contribution to the field was the publication of a comprehensive book based on papers presented at the conference, which illustrated a number of the Museum's recent acquisitions with original upholstery.[9]

Even as planning for the upholstery conference began, a much larger variety of scholars specializing in seventeenth-century America were collaborating on a special exhibition to celebrate the 350th anniversary of the founding of the Massachusetts Bay Colony in 1980. Prominent among these were David Hall, a scholar in seventeenth-century intellectual history and advisor on a successful research grant from the National Endowment for the Humanities, and Abbott Lowell Cummings, who had just published the definitive book on timber frame houses of seventeenth-century Massachusetts.[10] In 1977 Robert F. Trent joined the staff as a special research associate with responsibility for coordinating all aspects of the exhibition and catalogue. Extensive fieldwork in the research stage ferreted out a remarkable number of objects of the highest quality, some of them familiar and some new discoveries. Part of the fieldwork was undertaken by Robert St. George, who also made major contributions to the exhibition and its catalogue. Never before had a special loan exhibition brought such a compelling and important group of New England objects for the Museum's collections. The exhibition and a three-volume catalogue, both funded by the National Endowment for the Humanities and Fidelity Management and Research, shed new light on many different aspects of seventeenth-century culture. Hereafter, this institution became one the richest resources for the study and enjoyment of art of this era. Holdings of furniture had increased by about a third and paintings for the period tripled.

The trestle table was one of the most important forms of seventeenth-century furniture missing from the collection until we purchased an example with a Medfield provenance (3). The Museum had never sought out such vernacular furniture, which had little in the way of ornament to thrill the seeker of high arts. Aesthetic dimensions were only measurable by the table's overall proportions, division of articulated parts, and general utilitarian workmanship. Other similar "plain" acquisitions included a turned bedstead (1978.379) and a trundle bed (1977.801) and a pair of wrought iron andirons made in the late seventeenth century in Rhode Island, given by Mr.and Mrs. Samuel Robinson III (1979.379).

Other decorative arts objects of the first colonial period were hardly plain. A cabinet case of boxes made by the Mason Messinger shop in Boston between 1660 and 1700 (1982.16); a carved and painted chest made in Portsmouth, New Hampshire, in 1685 (1978.382); and a joined chest (4) with elaborate turnings made by the Symonds Shop of Salem, Massachusetts, at the end of the century all demonstrate that seventeenth-century American art was colorful and ornamental. No longer could the first settlers be represented as dull colonists with a sensuously repressed culture.

Jubilee 350, a city-organized celebration, included seventeenth-century craft demonstrations, theater performances, and music on Boston Common. With support from the Northeastern Retail Lumberman's Association, the curatorial staff oversaw the erection of a faithful replica of the original central section of the Fairbanks house (my ancestral home) built in Dedham in 1637. Joy Cattanach, a curatorial assistant, directed this project, which was coordinated with activities mounted by Plimoth Plantation and other New England historic agencies.

After the closing of the seventeenth-century exhibition, Joy Cattanach (now Smith) plunged into a new project, collaborating with the Twentieth Century Department curator Kenworth W. Moffett, his assistant Deborah M. Emerson, and myself to mount an exhibition entitled "Directions in Contemporary American Ceramics." Featuring works by fifteen artists covering a wide spectrum of artistic viewpoints, the exhibition was accompanied by a catalogue, and coincided with the 1984 Boston meetings of the National Council on Education for the Ceramic Arts and the International Academy of Ceramics.[11] Several pieces by artists in this exhibition were purchased with funds provided by Mary-Louise Meyer, including a raku bowl by Wayne Higby (47), vessels by Laura Andreson (44), and a stoneware lidded jar by Robert Turner (exh. no. 106).

These acquisitions of 1984 represent only a few of the major works by contemporary ceramic artists acquired through donations in recent years. In 1982 Donald O. Reichert of Springfield, Massachusetts, willed twenty works (1982.249-268) by American ceramic artists including Otto and Gertrud Natzler, Toshiko Takaezu, William Wyman and many other major artists. Mr. and Mrs. Stephen D. Paine were donors of a major work by Peter Voulkus and a handsome porcelain teapot by David Davidson.

Earlier, in 1973, Mr. and Mrs. William White Howells, who have also consistently donated important ceramic works, gave a prehistoric Pueblo bowl (1973.160) that developed staff interest in intensive collecting of Native American pottery, both contemporary and prehistoric. A decade later, in 1984 and 1985, an anonymous friend of the department sponsored two field trips to the Southwest with the explicit purpose of collecting contemporary Pueblo pottery. That beginning has both attracted several donations of Southwestern pottery and encouraged the development of prehistoric collections as evidenced by selections in this exhibition.[12]

While most of the hundreds of examples of contemporary American ceramics recently acquired have yet to find adequate viewing space in the Museum galleries, it would be curatorially irresponsible to let one of the most energetic movements in recent American art go uncollected simply because no one in the 1930s, when the old decorative art wing was built, anticipated the increased demand for space. Each generation needs to build space for its own collections as new collecting horizons develop.

In recent years one of the most exciting collecting arenas has been the late nineteenth-and early twentieth-century American arts of the Arts and Crafts movement. Wendy Kaplan, a member of the seventeenth-century exhibition team, wrote funding proposals and served as the research associate for the 1987 exhibition, "The Art that is Life': The Arts & Crafts Movement in America, 1875-1920." This exhibition and a handsome, award-winning catalogue involved collaboration of several writer/scholars and was funded by the National Endowment for the Humanities and Fidelity Management and Research, with additional support from the Luce Fund for Scholarship in American Art and the J. Paul Getty Trust.[13] The exhibition toured museums in Los Angeles, Detroit, and New York.

The exhibition acted as a catalyst in the marketplace; prices soared even during the run of the show. Anticipating this, staffmembers had already made serious acquisitions in the Arts and Crafts field, including a marvelous collection of works (1979.181-190) by silversmith Arthur Stone of Gardner, Massachusetts. Accompanying the objects were Stone's personal design library, his notes and his business records, all donated by Miss Alma Bent.

Although exhibitions stimulate or summarize knowledge and chart new directions in collecting, the institution's older collections remain vital. In 1983 and 1984 two major pieces of early New England silver were given by Jane Bortman Larus who has been a departmental friend for years.[14] Jane's gifts have included a handsome teapot made in Boston by Benjamin Burt in 1763 (54) and a silver-handled sword (53) made by Jacob Hurd of Boston in 1735 for Richard Hazen, a wealthy landholder of Haverhill, Massachusetts.

The most important group of American silver to enter the Museum's collection since 1913 came in 1984: twelve pieces of early Massachusetts church silver (1984.204-215) from the Second Congregational Society (now known as the Unitarian Universalist Church) in Marblehead, Massachusetts. The collection includes a monumental baptismal basin by John Coney, Boston's foremost early eighteenth-century goldsmith, and a pair of tall flagons made by John Burt (48). This impressive assembly of plate suggests the importance of Congregational worship in the daily lives of membership and carries with it today the memory of the institution for which it was made.

Community memory and identity were strong components of a 1984 exhibition honoring Bertram K. and Nina Fletcher Little of Brookline and Essex, Massachusetts, foremost collectors of early American folk, provincial, and popular art. The exhibition celebrated the publication of *Little by Little, Six Decades of Collecting American Decorative Arts*, written by Nina, a long-time friend and Honorary Fellow for Research.[15]

Additions to the Museum's traditional strengths of eighteenth-century American furniture have fundamentally changed our knowledge about the development of style. A series of monumental case pieces included in this exhibition illustrate that point. Each of them reveals important information not only about stylistic changes, but about shop practices and patronage between 1715 and 1782. This display highlights some of the most spectacular high-style furniture acquired in the past twenty years, but not all furniture accessions are rooted in English traditions. The scope of the collection has been extended to include furniture that displays other national origins. For example, a buffet (20) from Vincennes, Indiana, is expressive of French culture of the upper Mississippi Valley region at the end of the eighteenth century, and a recently acquired wardrobe from Fredericksburg, Texas (21), shows evidence of Germanic background. This marvel of frontier furniture was donated by Mrs. Charles L. Bybee who loaned several examples of Texas furniture to the Far West exhibition in 1975/6, and, in 1981, donated a rare pair of Boston-made side chairs (1981.16, 17) with Japanned decoration.

From 1980 until 1987 staff and consultants worked toward the publication of a book on the permanent collection of the American sculpture in the Museum.[16] As the book progressed, several pieces of sculpture were donated. Among these was a handsome bronze figure of Nathan Hale (1984.501) by Bela Lyon Pratt (1867-1917), donated by Trustee and Visitor Joseph Pellegrino and former Museum President George Seybolt. A pair of small bronze figures of Art and Science (1979.386, 387), Pratt's sketches for the heroic bronzes at the front of the historic Boston Public Library, were given by Jo Ann and Julian Gantz, Jr. Seven works by Richard H. Recchia (1888-1983) came as a bequest of the sculptor through the advice of sculptor Walker Hancock of Lanesville. Hancock himself made two important gifts of his own work to the Museum. The *Fallen Boxer* (1980.425), which is a bronze made in 1934, and the original plaster model for the *Head of an Angel* (36), which was cast in bronze as part of the Pennsylvania Railroad War Memorial unveiled in 1952 at the Thirtieth Street Station, Philadelphia. Katharine Lane Weems (1899-1989) gave several pieces of her sculpture during her lifetime, the most important being a bronze figure she entitled *Revolt* (35). Also, she endowed the fourth curatorial chair in the history of the Museum — the chair I hold in her name frees funds to hire an assistant curator with a specialty in sculpture. We thus were fortunate to hire Lauretta Dimmick, formerly of the Metropolitan Museum of Art. Following Weems's death in 1989, the entire sculptural contents of her studio in Manchester, Massachusetts, came to the Museum with gifts to many other departments and to the Museum School. Collecting early twentieth-century American sculpture continues through the support of Visitors Jean S. and Frederic A. Sharf. They made it possible to recently acquire, among other works, a beautiful small bronze, *The Debutante* (34) by Herbert Adams, a former president of the National Sculpture Society.

The field of decorative arts made in the 1920s and 1930s is collected aggressively by department Visitor John Axelrod, who has given several objects made in the 1920s and 1930s, loaned works that fill an entire gallery, and promised to bequeath his entire collection. An important ceramic work — *The Jazz Bowl* by Victor Schreckengost (42) represents the vitality and visual excitement of art in the Axelrod collection. It is one of the most recent acquisitions presented in this exhibition, generously donated in part, in response to this exhibition.

A compelling exhibition of works by Tiffany & Co. celebrated the 150th anniversary of the company's founding. Department Visitor Charles H. Carpenter and Tiffany & Co. archivist Janet Zapata wrote a fine catalogue for the exhibition. The silver pitcher on the cover, made for display at the 1876 Centennial Exposition in Philadelphia, was later given to the Museum and became the first American decorative arts object to enter the collection (77.61). I have often cited that first acquisition as a way of convincing skeptics of the tradition and importance of collecting contemporary decorative arts in this country.

In recent years the staff has vigorously acquired many wonderful examples of contemporary American furniture. Acquired through the NEA-funded "Please Be Seated Program," works by Wendell Castle, the late George Nakashima, Tage Frid and Judy McKie grace the galleries of the Museum as permanent collection objects and visitor seating. When NEA funds for contemporary furniture faltered, new life was provided by Ronald and Anne Abramson of Washington, D.C., who since 1985 have donated several works including a visually arresting chair of wood and metal (1985.732) by Jay Stanger of Charlestown, Massachusetts. The Abramsons also donated a magnificent bench (28) by Rosanne Somerson and several other important pieces of case furniture, signalling a new collecting direction that went beyond seating. The Museum also amassed a fine collection of wooden turned vessels that started with works by Bob Stocksdale and James Prestini and enlarged in scope to include the master turners David Ellsworth, Ed Moulthrop, and Rude Osolnik.

The first major exhibition of contemporary crafts in all media, "The Eloquent Object," came from the Philbrook Museum, Tulsa, in 1988.[17] This complex exhibition involved eleven catalogue contributors including myself and was installed at the Museum under the supervision of curatorial assistant Jeannine Falino.

A second travelling exhibition, "John La Farge," arrived in early 1988. Handsomely installed under the guidance of Lauretta Dimmick, the show featured La Farge's oils, watercolors, and stained glass, and fostered new appreciation of his sense of color and composition. It was an important exhibition for Boston and pointed out that his greatest accomplishments were his stained glass windows and monumental mural designs, rather than his easel paintings.

Even while "The Eloquent Object" and "John La Farge" were on view, a more focused contemporary display was being developed by Edward S. Cooke, Jr. In 1989 the outstanding exhibition, "New American Furniture: The Second Generation of American Studio Furnituremakers" opened. The catalogue was written from a historical as well as contemporary viewpoint and recorded the process of conception, design, and construction of twenty-six craftsmen/artists who used Museum objects as sources of inspiration for works produced for this exhibition.[18] The exhibition traveled from the Renwick Gallery in Washington, D.C., to Cincinnati and Oakland. Several important works in that exhibition are destined for the Museum's collections.

The first example of monumental studio/craftsmen metal entered the collection in 1989 through funding by the NEA, matched with donations made by Seminarians. This is a breathtaking plant stand by Albert Paley (65), that needs no plant to complete its composition. It is a remarkable performance of metalsmithing and is a unique work that stands at a transition point in Paley's career.

Just what the future holds for collecting the American arts of design, crafts, and sculpture at the Museum will depend only in part on the vision of the staff here. It will also depend on those who have the courage to face the marketplace, to assist the Museum, and to call attention to works of remarkable originality or quality. Words of advice from a friend, dealer or even a total stranger have opened remarkable pathways in the past and will continue to do so. Staff interests, exhibitions, publications and the circle of friends that continues to expand is only a part of the collecting story.[19] Changing circumstances in the lives of individuals and communities also make important works available. Sometimes it becomes the task of staff to save works from obscurity or vandalism and conserve them. Evidence of that work surrounds the visitor to this exhibition as the invaluable talents of the furniture conservation lab headed by Robert Walker and assisted by Susan Odell Walker and Letitia Stevens are manifest in every piece of furniture displayed here.

The most gratifying aspect of collecting is sharing and discovering the interests of many individuals who enjoy American arts. Institutional collecting is quite unlike private collecting. An institution's task is to fulfill the needs of many different individuals, constituencies and generations over time, while an individual's search is necessarily finite and only expressive of a single viewpoint. The moment institutional collection growth and change ceases will signal a generation without a distinct aesthetic will. At that time we might as well, sadly, finish the Museum's facade.

NOTES

1. At the time I was the associate curator at the Winterthur Museum in Delaware and responsible for developing that institution's research facility and directing the conservation program.

2. When Cerbone retired in 1976, an English trained cabinetmaker, Robert G. Walker, was appointed head of the lab. The furniture lab has proven an effective training ground for several important individuals in the field, including Alan Breed, Brian Considine, Alec Graham, Sharon Odekirk, and Marc Williams.

3. Curatorial Visiting Committees comprise collectors, museum professionals, and long-time friends and patrons who are closely concerned with the Department's welfare and development. Approximately 45 people serve on our Visiting Committee, whose trustee chairmen have been Edward C. Johnson III, Mrs. Henry R. Guild, Jr., and Joseph P. Pellegrino. Mrs. Henry K. Bramhall, Jr. and Elaine Wilde have been co-chairs. (The Department's record of Visitor loyalty is outstanding; a complete list of is published in every annual report.)

4. Walter Muir Whitehill, Bock Jobe, Jonathan Fairbanks, et. al., *Boston Furniture of the Eighteenth Century* (Boston, The Colonial Society of Massachusetts, 1974).

5. For a discussion of the refurnishing of the Oak Hill Rooms, see Museum of Fine Arts *Bulletin*, vol. 83, 1983, pp. 1-60.

6. *American Pewter in the Museum of Fine Arts, Boston*, Museum of Fine Arts, Boston, 1974.

7. Eight authors contributed to the catalogue, *Frontier America: The Far West*, which was sponsored through matching grants from the National Endowment for the Arts and Philip Morris Incorporated on behalf of Marlboro. Six writers contributed to the catalogue *Paul Revere's Boston: 1735-1818*, with special collaboration with Stephen T. Riley, Director of the Massachusetts Historical Society, who poured countless hours into developing the exhibition.

8. Jan Seidler, "A Critical Reappraisal of the Career of William Wetmore Story (1819-1895), American Sculptor and Man of Letters," Ph.D. diss, Boston University, 1985.

9. Had it not been for the leadership of Robert McNeil, President of the Barra Foundation, and for the persuasive editorial and scholarly talents of Edward S. Cooke, Jr., the prize-winning book *Upholstery in America & Europe from the Seventeenth Century to World War I* (New York: Barra Foundation and W.W. Norton, 1987), would never have been produced. It had a complicated genesis with twenty-two contributors, spanning both sides of the Atlantic.

10. David Hall, who was the first director of the American and New England Studies Program at Boston University, offered critical insight throughout the exhibition planning. He also insured that qualified graduate students from the program were continually exposed to MFA collections as interns or researchers. Abbott Cummings, then Director for the Society for the Preservation of New England Antiquities, and now the Charles F. Montgomery Professor, American Decorative Arts, History of Art, at Yale University, gave invaluable encouragement and guidance to the facsimile house building project and continues to serve as a Visitor to the department. His book, *The Framed Houses of Massachusetts Bay, 1625-1727* (Cambridge, Mass.: Harvard University Press, 1979), served as the scholarly foundation for the exhibition.

11. Fairbanks, Moffett, Emerson and Smith, *Directions in Contemporary American Ceramics*. The exhibition included works by Laura Andreson, Robert Arneson, Rudy Autio, Walter Darby Bannard, Anthony Caro, Stephen DeStaebler, Friedel Dzubas, Viola Frey, Wayne Higby, Margie Hughto, Jun Kaneko, Richard Shaw, Rudolf Staffel, Robert Turner, and Betty Woodman.

12. Laura Andreson, noted ceramic artist of California, donated a splendid collection of twenty-three examples of Pueblo pottery (1984.613-636), which she acquired in the 1930s.

13. Wendy Kaplan et. al., *"The Art That is Life": The Arts & Crafts Movement in America, 1875-1920*, Museum of Fine Arts, Boston, 1987.

14. Her father, Mark Bortman, was an important collector of silver who, in the 1940s, engineered the campaign for contributions that obtained the famous Revere Liberty Bowl for the Museum.

15. Nina Fletcher Little, *Little by Little, Six Decades of Collecting American Decorative Arts* (New York: E.P. Dutton, 1984).

16. Greenthal, Kozol, Ramirez, *American Figurative Sculpture in the Museum of Fine Arts, Boston*. Jan Seidler Ramirez, Kathryn Greenthal and Paula M. Kozol wrote entries on sculpture in the collection, and biographies on each of the artists. The volume was funded by Mr. and Mrs. Henry R. Guild, Jr., with a supporting grant from the National Endowment for the Humanities, and included scientific analysis of the bronzes by the Museum's Research Laboratory.

17. Marcia Manhart, Tom Manhart, et. al., *The Eloquent Object, The Evolution of American Art in Craft Media Since 1945* (Tulsa, Oklahoma: The Philbrook Museum of Art, 1987).

18. Edward S. Cooke, Jr., *New American Furniture: The Second Generation of Studio Furnituremakers* (Boston: Museum of Fine Arts, Boston, 1989).

19. Successful curators collect collectors who have spent their lifetimes and fortunes gathering the finest works, often in specialized areas. While it is often said that such superb collectors have a "great eye," excellence in collecting is actually dependent on cultivated taste, expert knowledge, and intuition based on experience. Great collecting is communicative and culture-driven unless one simply inherits masterworks from the past. In a sense, the Museum does both. For my views on this see "A Room Not Filled" *Studio Potter* vol. 17, no. 1, December 1988, pp. 37-39. For connoisseurship guidelines see Charles F. Montgomery, "Some Remarks on the Practice and Science of Connoisseurship," Walpole Society Note Book (The Walpole Society, 1962), pp. 56-69.

8. *Desk-and-Bookcase,* 1760-1780.

15. Attributed to John Finlay or Hugh Finlay, *Grecian Couch,* 1820-1840

37. American China Manufactory
Fruit Basket, 1771-1772

42. Cowan Pottery Studio
Punch Bowl from the "Jazz Bowl"
series, 1931, designed and decorated by
Viktor Schreckengost

45. Brother Thomas (Thomas Bezanson)
Vase, 1980

71. John La Farge, *Morning Glories,*
1877-1878

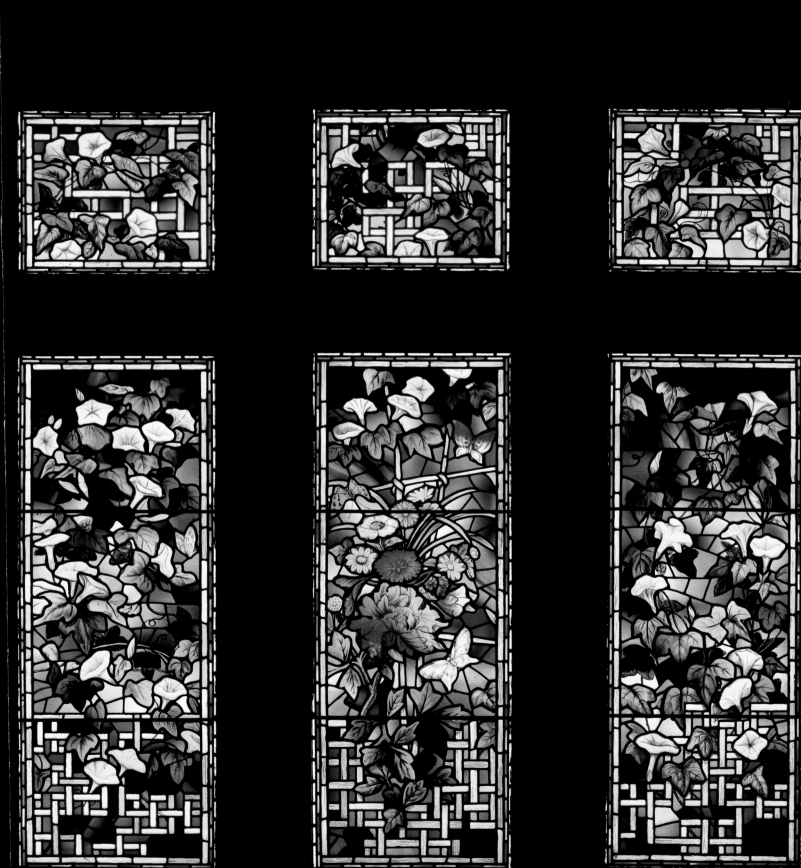

73. Dan Dailey, *"Dense Growth" Vase from Science Fiction Series,* 1984-1988

80. Lillian Salvadore, *Olla*, 1984

1.

Leather Great Chair (exh. no. 17)
Boston, 1665-1680
Oak, maple; original upholstery foundation,
leather cover, and brass nails
H. 38 in., W. 23⅝ in., D. 16⅜ in.

Seth K. Sweetser Fund 1977.711

In the last half of the seventeenth century, upholstered leather chairs were the most fashionable form of seating furniture for the well-
to-do merchants, magistrates, and ministers
of colonial New England. Leather chairs,
and related turkey-work and serge-covered
frames, retained their preeminence until 1695
when high-backed, caned, carved chairs in a
baroque style became the most sought-after
seating. Although some of the materials such
as leather and the grass stuffing were available
locally, the imported webbing, sackcloth, and

brass nails and the time necessary to stuff and
cover the chairs made them expensive. In fact,
upholstery remained a luxury trade based in
densely populated urban areas until the early
nineteenth century.[1]

This leather great chair, the only armed
version known to have survived, was originally owned by Zerubbabel Endicott (1635-
1683), a Salem surgeon and son of Governor
John Endicott (1588-1665). The provenance
and such typical mid-century English features
as the wide frame, leather-wrapped back and
front posts, and square-dimensioned arms
with chamfered edges suggest that this example was made between 1665 and 1680. It retains its original foundation (consisting of
linen webbing, linen sackcloth, and grass) and
leather cover, but the cushion is a modern
fabrication based on print sources. The arms,
the height of the cushioned seat, and the ex-

pense of the materials for the cushion distinguish the Endicott chair as the throne of a
patriarch.[2]

E.S.C.

1. For more thorough treatments of leather chairs
and other chairs of the period, see Benno Forman,
American Seating Furniture, 1630-1730 (New
York: W.W. Norton, 1988), esp. pp. 195-228; Robert F. Trent, "17th-Century Upholstery in Massachusetts," in Edward S. Cooke, Jr., ed., *Upholstery
in America & Europe from the Seventeenth Century
to World War I* (New York: W.W. Norton, 1987),
pp. 39-50; and Robert F. Trent, "A New Model
Army of Cromwellian Chairs," *Maine Antique Digest* (September 1986), Section C, pp. 10-16.

2. For more on the Endicott chair, see Robert F.
Trent, "The Endicott Chairs," *Essex Institute Historical Collections* 114, no. 2 (April 1978), pp. 103-
119.

2.

Chest of Drawers with Doors (exh. no. 18)
New Haven, Connecticut, 1670-1700
Oak, walnut, cedar, pine
H. 36⅜ in., W. 44⅜ in., D. 22¾ in.

Edwin E. Jack Fund 1980.274

The town of New Haven was founded in
1638 by a group of non-conformist London
merchants and their minister, John Daven-
port. While the group sought to establish the
strictest form of Puritanism in New England,
they also sought to preserve aspects of their
London built environment. Stephen Good-
year, for example, organized a group of
London craftsmen to move to New Haven in
1639. Among the immigrants were two joiners, William Russell (1612-1648/1649) and
William Gibbons (here by 1640-1689), who
apparently began to produce London-style
furniture in the New Haven area.[1]

This chest of drawers with doors and a cupboard at the Yale University Art Gallery are
the most significant works made by New Haven joiners. It is one of only two surviving colonial examples of the complex storage form
in which doors conceal some of the drawers.
The geometric inlay of walnut sapwood and
heartwood and the applied architectonic spin-
dles of cedar do not appear on the work of
any other colonial shop but do resemble English work. The construction of the New Haven chest also manifests closer ties with
London conventions: all of the given members of the frame have been left unplaned on
the inner surface, the rails are wide, and the
joiner used two thin boards for each of the
side panels. An ornamental emphasis on the
front accompanied the parsimonious use of
wood. These aspects of flashy low-end
London work do not appear on the work of
the other prominent London-influenced shop
in New England, the Mason-Messinger shop
of Boston. The Boston work, which includes
the second chest of drawers with doors, features thicker finished framing members, larger
planks, and no inlaid decoration.[2]
E.S.C.

2. For a more detailed analysis of the New Haven
chest, see Jonathan L. Fairbanks and Robert F.
Trent, eds. *New England Begins: The Seventeenth
Century* (Boston: Museum of Fine Arts, Boston,
1982), vol. 3, pp. 524-526. Gerald W.R. Ward cau-
tions scholars not to attribute the New Haven
pieces to a Russell-Gibbons shop: *American Case
Furniture in the Mabel Brady Garvan and Other
Collections at Yale University* (New Haven: Yale
University Art Gallery, 1988), pp. 101-102 and
377-379.

1. Patricia E. Kane, *Furniture of the New Haven
Colony: The Seventeenth-Century Style* (New Haven, Connecticut: The New Haven Colony Historical Society, 1973).

Attributed to Benjamin Clark
(1644-1724)

3.
Board and Trestles (exh. no. 19)
Medfield, Massachusetts, 1690-1720
Silver maple, white pine
H. 26³/₁₆ in., w. 24³/₄ in., L. 108½ in.

Helen and Alice Colburn Fund and Frederick
Brown Fund 1980.446

The trestle table form calls forth a wide range
of associations, from the Last Supper to medieval interiors, early New England society, and
Shaker simplicity. While few early American
examples survive, its simple, honest construction, and its use as the focal point in a seventeenth-century hall have made it a favorite
form among collectors of Early American furniture. In colonial inventories such long communal tables were referred to as a board and
trestles or table and trestles, indicating that
the long boards of the top simply rested on
the trestles. The lack of securing hardware enabled the table to be dismantled and stored
more easily. In the late seventeenth century,
tables with leaved oval tops and ornately
turned legs replaced the board and trestle as
the favored flexible table.[1]

The board and trestles owned by Joseph
Clark III (1664-1731), possibly made by his
uncle Benjamin Clark (1644-1724), exhibits
typical joinery of the period: pinned mortise-
and-tenon joints and subtle chamfers with
lamb's tongue and diamond stops on the tie
beam and trestles. These decorative details resemble those on the beams of the Peak house
in Medfield, built by Benjamin Clark in 1676.
Originally cleats at either end of the two top
boards secured the boards together, but the
cleats have been lost, and the boards were
nailed instead to the trestles.[2]
E.S.C.

1. Irving W. Lyon, *The Colonial Furniture of New
England* (Boston: Houghton, Mifflin and Company,
1891), pp.189-201; and Wallace Nutting, *Furniture
of the Pilgrim Century, 1620-1720* (Boston: Marshall Jones, 1921), pp. 340-386.
2. Jonathan L. Fairbanks and Robert F. Trent, *New
England Begins: The Seventeenth Century* (Boston:
Museum of Fine Arts, Boston, 1982), vol. 3, pp.
213-214.

Attributed to the Symonds shop

4.
Chest with Drawer (exh. no. 20)
Salem, Massachusetts, 1660-1700
Oak, maple, walnut, cedar
H. 28⅞ in., W. 46 in., D. 20¾ in.

Frank B. Bemis Fund 1984.88

The earliest joiners in colonial America preserved the regional traditions in which they
had been trained before they immigrated.
John Symonds (1595-1671), for example,
learned the craft in Great Yarmouth, Norfolk,
before coming to Salem in 1636. He brought
with him knowledge of and experience in a
very advanced Mannerist style that featured
architectural compositions, applied intricate
moldings and architectural details like corbels
and keystones, and carved caryatids and atlantes. In Salem, Symonds adapted this tradition, emphasizing the compositional elements
and the articulation of facades with moldings
but rejecting the carved elements. Over three
generations, the Symonds shop continued to
develop its own expression, drawing upon the
Great Yarmouth style, but also incorporating
elements of Boston work in the late seventeenth century.[1]

This chest with drawer belongs to a group
of case furniture in which dated examples
range from 1676 to 1701. It was thus probably the work of John Symonds's sons James
(1633-1714) or Samuel (1638-1722), but it
possesses typical Salem features without the
influence of Boston joinery from the last quarter of the seventeenth century. Some chests
made by the second generation of the Symonds feature Doric columns and bipartite
drawer fronts typical of contemporary Boston
work, but this chest has the distinctive Salem
multiple urn-and-reel turnings and the tripartite drawer front. The overall organization of
the chest's facade demonstrates the Great Yarmouth architectural composition: the base,
waist, and frieze moldings represent the surbase, base, and capital of a column; and the
applied moldings on the drawer align with
those on the case and with the triglyphs in the
uppermost rail. The English regional tradition
can also be seen in elaborate mitred moldings
and octagonal sunburst that give the panels
linear and textural vitality. The joiner used

red cedar for the moldings, black walnut for
the plaques, and ebonized maple to provide
differences in color.[2]

E.S.C.

1. For a thorough discussion of the Symonds shops,
see Robert F. Trent, "The Symonds Shops of Essex
County, Massachusetts," in Francis J. Puig and
Michael Conforti, eds., *The American Craftsman
and the European Tradition, 1620-1820* (Minneapolis: The Minneapolis Institute of Arts, 1989), pp.
23-41.
2. For more on this chest, see Jonathan L. Fairbanks
and Robert F. Trent, eds., *New England Begins: The
Seventeenth Century* (Boston: Museum of Fine
Arts, Boston, 1982), vol. 3, pp. 526-527.

5.
Chest-on-Chest (exh. no. 24)
Boston, Massachusetts, 1715-1725
Black walnut, burl walnut veneer, eastern
white pine
H. 70¾ in., w. 42¼ in., D. 21½ in.

Gift of a Friend of the Department of American Decorative Arts and Sculpture and Otis Norcross Fund 1986.240

Considerable attention has been focused upon Boston furniture of the seventeenth and mid-eighteenth centuries, but comparatively little is known about the town's furniture production in the first quarter of the eighteenth century. While some William-and-Mary style pieces of furniture have been attributed to Boston, there has been no body of furniture comparable in quality and fashion to the silver made at the time. Such an inconsistency is all the more striking because Boston experienced considerable commercial growth in the early eighteenth century, and written and material evidence indicates that its leading citizens invested considerable sums in stylish architecture and furnishings.

This chest-on-chest is the keystone to understanding the development of early eighteenth-century furniture in Boston. At first glance, one would mistake it for an English example: its middling height, canted fluted pilasters, pull-out folding board, two upper drawers in the lower section, and recessed semicircular star inlay in the lower drawer are all features typical of English work in the Georgian style of the second decade of the eighteenth century. The veneered molding, the thin stock and grain orientation of the drawer construction, and the full-depth dustboards between drawers are also characteristic of English construction at that time.

However, this chest-on-chest was owned in the eighteenth century by the Warland family of Cambridge, and was made by an English-trained cabinetmaker working in Boston. The main exterior wood is black walnut (the American species *Juglans nigra* rather than the English *Juglans regia*), and the sole secondary wood is white pine (not the combination of deal, oak, or beech found on English examples). Analysis of the original dirt and particles located along the underside of the bracket feet revealed no English pollen but did indicate that the chest resided originally in an urban location in Massachusetts or Rhode Island. This chest-on-chest thus demonstrates that the efforts to find Boston William-and-Mary furniture may result in an only partial picture of the Boston furniture craft at that time. It may prove more rewarding to look instead for early Georgian examples constructed by recent immigrants. Like the silver trade, the furniture craft in the early eighteenth century was dramatically influenced by

English-trained artisans who made furniture in the Georgian style in which they had been trained. As transmitters of recent English fashion, they enjoyed considerable patronage in anglophilic Boston.[1]

E.S.C.

1. For a more detailed analysis of the chest, see Edward S. Cooke, Jr., "The Warland Chest: Early Georgian Furniture in Boston," *Maine Antiques Digest* (March 1987), section C, pp. 10-13.

6.

Clothespress (exh. no. 28)
Boston, Massachusetts, 1740-1750
Mahogany, chestnut, white pine
H. 90¾ in., w. 45 in., D. 22¼ in.

Gift of Friends of the Department of American Decorative Arts and Sculpture 1987.254

One of the most visually powerful yet little understood Boston furniture forms of the eighteenth century was the clothespress. Few examples exist, probably because Boston cabinetmakers made far greater numbers of high chests of drawers in the second quarter of the eighteenth century and chest-on-chests and desk-and-bookcases in the third quarter. The clothespress reflected an English orientation of the maker or owner.

This particular clothespress is one of four that feature a closed ogee pediment based upon Anglo-Dutch prototypes, but the only one with an accurate provenance. Originally owned by the Boston merchant Gilbert Deblois, it was probably made in 1749 for his marriage to Ann Coffin. Deblois achieved considerable wealth before the Revolution. However, his staunch loyalism forced him to flee to England for the duration of the war, leaving his family and possessions in Boston.[1]

The Deblois clothespress reflects an English outlook circumscribed by a provincial environment. Its configuration of drawers behind doors above a chest of drawers, cornice shape, folding board, complex mid-molding, and drawer construction make reference to the English high style of the early eighteenth century, yet other features reflect local conventions. The use of solid mahogany rather than walnut veneer for the primary wood, and chestnut rather than oak for the drawer linings distinguishes the Deblois example from its earlier English prototypes. The shop that produced the Deblois clothespress and other large case furniture seemed to enjoy the patronage of many well-to-do merchants and anglophiles who were succeeding in the volatile economic climate of the mid-1700s. These patronage patterns provide material evidence that Massachusetts became anglicized during the course of the early eighteenth century, a critical precondition of its subsequent fight for independence. In fact, between 1730 and 1760 the local officials and the merchants shared a strong common identity as associates in the English empire. They no longer felt dependent and thus were outraged by the Crown's violation of their rights in the 1760s.
E.S.C.

1. For a more extensive discussion of the Deblois clothespress, see Edward S. Cooke, Jr., "Boston Clothespresses of the Mid-Eighteenth Century," *Journal of the Museum of Fine Arts, Boston* 1 (1989), pp. 75-95.

7.

Chest-on-Chest (exh. no. 31)
Boston, Massachusetts, about 1770
Mahogany, white pine
H. 83 in., W. 45 in., D. 21 in.

Bequest of Amelia Peabody 1984.520

During the third quarter of the eighteenth century, Boston cabinetmakers relied on two different conventions to produce elaborate, decorative case furniture. Rather than make extensive use of carving or inlay, Boston furnituremakers concentrated on the outline of the form itself. They either shaped the sides to produce the swelling bombé or shaped the front facade to produce the alternately projecting and recessing blockfront form. While the bombé forms were usually the most expensive pieces of case furniture, the craftsman could add certain extras such as carving or distinctive hardware to the blockfront to increase its value.

Such an embellished blockfront form is this chest-on-chest, originally owned by the cloth merchant Ebenezer Storer, Jr. (1734-1809). The inventory of his sumptuously furnished house on Sudbury Street listed a "case of drawers $10" in the parlor chamber. The chest reflects the taste and means of its owner in the richness of the shaped mahogany, the folding board between the upper and lower sections (an English convention rarely seen on Boston furniture from the third quarter of the eighteenth century), the elaborately carved shell and rosettes, and fashionable Chinoiserie fire gilt brasses imported from Birmingham, England. Also owned by Storer were a serpentine-front bombe chest of drawers with fire gilt brasses and a pair of side chairs with elaborately carved crests and splats; together, they identify the merchant as one of Boston's leaders in fashion.[1] Although a chest-on-chest with a similar carved shell bears the label of Benjamin Frothingham (1734-1809) of Charlestown, differences in drawer construction, molding profiles, and template patterns for the feet and tympanum of the Storer example suggest a different shop. The carver may have been a specialist who worked for several shops including that of Frothingham. Initial work on Boston carvers has begun and will need to be carried on in conjunction with analysis of case construction in order to sort out the intricate relationships between various cabinetmakers' shops and carvers.[2]
E.S.C.

1. Clifford Shipton, *Sibley's Harvard Graduates* (Boston: Massachusetts Historical Society, 1962), vol. 12, pp. 208-214; Suffolk County Probate Court, docket 22829, vol. 105, pp. 202-203. The chest is illustrated in *Paul Revere's Boston* (Boston: Museum of Fine Arts, Boston, 1976), p. 76; and the chairs are in a private collection in Boston.

2. For similar shells, see *Boston Furniture of the Eighteenth Century* (Boston: The Colonial Society of Massachusetts, 1974), p. vi; Richard A. Bourne auction catalog (May 17, 1983), no. 325; and Richard A. Bourne auction catalog (November 26, 1983), no. 340. On the need for additional study of Boston carvers, see Christopher Monkhouse and Thomas Michie, *American Furniture in Pendleton House* (Providence: Rhode Island School of Design, 1986), pp. 78-79; and Luke Beckerdite, "Carving Practices in Eighteenth-Century Boston," *Old-Time New England* 72 (1987), pp. 123-162.

8. (color plate)
Desk-and-Bookcase (exh. no. 32)
Salem, Massachusetts, 1760-1780
Mahogany, white pine
H. 99¾ in., W. 46½ in., D. 25 in.

Gift of Lucy Davis Donovan, Emily Lincoln
Lewis and Mary Lowell Warren in Memory
of their Mother, Mary Lowell Davis
1989.308

It is rare that monumental pieces of eighteenth-century American case furniture have
remained unknown or are given to museums.
A century of active collecting and publishing
and the lure of high values have brought
many important pieces to public attention.
The rising prices of the past decade, coupled
with shrinking tax incentives for charitable
contributions of art objects, has slowed donations to museum collections.

The Lowell desk-and-bookcase has traditionally been associated with Judge John
Lowell (1743-1802) and attributed to a Boston shop. However, new scholarship suggests
that a Salem shop made this monumental
piece of furniture. Branded "w c" on the top
edge of the cornice molding, the desk was
probably made originally for Lowell's
brother-in-law William Cabot, a Salem
merchant who owned two mahogany desk-
and-bookcases at his death in 1828, and subsequently inherited by his nephew the Reverend Charles Lowell (1787-1861). According
to family history, the desk-and-bookcase descended from Charles Lowell to James Russell
Lowell (1819-1891), to Mabel Lowell Burnett
(1847-1898), Esther Lowell Burnett Cunningham (1879-1966), and Mary Lowell Cunningham Davis (b. 1913).[1]

In the third quarter of the eighteenth century several cabinetmakers provided furniture
for Salem's leading families such as the
Cabots. Much of the shops' production related quite closely with Boston work of the
same period. Several case pieces have only recently been attributed to Henry Rust (1737-
1812). The Lowell desk-and-bookcase was
the ambitious work of yet another Salem cabinetmaker.[2] The engaged pilasters surmounting console bases on the lower section, the
carved decoration of the frieze on the upper
section, the full-width folding board that
doubles as a writing surface support and the
original gilding of the ball feet are rare on
coastal Massachusetts examples.[3]
E.S.C.

1. Cabot died single, and his trustees included his
nephew, the Reverend Charles Lowell. It seems
likely that Charles Lowell inherited a desk-and-
bookcase at this time. For genealogical information,
see the object folder, Department of American Decorative Arts and Sculpture, Museum of Fine Arts,
Boston; Delmar Lowell, *The Historic Genealogy of
the Lowells of America* (Rutland, Vermont: The
Tuttle Company, 1899); and Will of William Cabot

(1828), Docket 3842, Middlesex County Probate
Court, Cambridge, Massachusetts.

2. Rust used different templates for his feet and
brackets. Other features also reveal differing workmanship from that of Rust: a giant dovetail secures
the base molding to the carcass bottom, the bottom
blocking for the feet is not substantial and lacks the
angled cut on the rear block, the upper edges of the
drawer sides are merely rounded, the prospect door
is lined up with pins, and the pediment is supported
by two brackets. For information on Rust and the
furniture attributed to his shop, see Charles Venable, *American Furniture in the Bybee Collection*
(Austin: University of Texas Press, 1989), pp. 58-63.

3. Related pieces made in the same shop are a desk-
and-bookcase sold by John Walton, a desk sold by
Ginsburg and Levy, and a desk at the Museum of
Fine Arts: *Antiques* 72, no. 2 (August 1957), p. 96;
Antiques 60, no. 4 (October 1951), p. 244, and
Richard Randall, *American Furniture in the Museum of Fine Arts, Boston* (Boston: Museum of Fine
Arts, Boston, 1965), pp. 76-77. Section analysis of
the gilded areas by Richard Newman, Research Sci-
entist at the Museum of Fine Arts, indicated that
there was original gilding on the feet, with a more
recent gilding applied over it. The rosettes, originally ungilded, were also gilded at that time.

John Cogswell
(1738-1818)

9.
Chest-on-Chest (exh. no. 37)
Boston, Massachusetts, 1782
Mahogany, white pine
H. 89½ in., w. 43½ in., D. 23½ in.

Signed on inside surface of back board of
lower case: "J. Cogswel"
Signed on top of lower case: "Made by John /
Cogswell in midle street / Boston 1782"
William Francis Warren Fund. 1973.289

Elias Hasket Derby, the prominent Salem
merchant, commissioned at least five chest-
on-chests of exceptional merit in the late eighteenth century.[1] According to an accompanying document, this example was made by
John Cogswell for Derby's grandson John
Derby to take to Harvard when he entered in
1782.[2] Cogswell dated and signed the piece
twice.

Cogswell's Middle Street shop was only a
few blocks from the silversmith shop of contemporary Paul Revere in the artisan community of Boston's North End. From this community Cogswell likely found a carving
specialist to execute the exceptionally rich
work on the finials, Corinthian capitals, and
cabriole leg supports of this chest-on-chest.
Because similar carving details can be identified on Boston furniture made in other shops,
attributions cannot be made on the basis of
carving alone.[3]
R.J.M.

1. A second chest-on-chest traditionally attributed
to Samuel McIntire for design and some carving is
in the Museum's M. and M. Karolik Collection. In
the Garvan collection at the Yale University Art
Gallery is a chest-on-chest made in about 1791 by
Stephen Bedlam of Dorchester, Mass. The locations
of the two remaining chests are unknown.

2. Included with the chest is a typed card with the
inscription: Wardrobe/Made by John Cogswell,
Middle St. Boston/in 1782 for/Mrs Elias Haskett
Derby (Elizabeth Crowninshield)/for grandson John
Derby of Salem, when/he went to Harvard College./
Similar ones were made for each of her/
grandchildren.

3. Luke Beckerdite, "Carving Practices in Eighteenth-Century Boston," *Old-Time New England*,
(Boston: Society for the Preservation of New England Antiquities, 1987). See also Gilbert T. Vincent, "The Bombe Furniture of Boston," *Boston
Furniture of the Eighteenth Century* (Boston: The
Colonial Society of Massachusetts, 1972), pp. 137-
196.

10.

High Chest of Drawers (exh. no. 38)
Newtown, Connecticut, 1760-1780
Cherry, yellow poplar, oak
H. 82 in., W. 42½ in., D. 20¾ in.

Gift of a Friend of the Department of American Decorative Arts and Sculpture, Eddy Nicholson, the Arthur Tracy Cabot Fund, and Anonymous Gift 1988.16

Eighteenth-century Connecticut furniture has fascinated collectors, curators, and writers for its idiosyncratic styles and aberrations of urban fashion. A popular adage states "If it's odd and cherry, then it's Connecticut." This fascination, however, has not been translated into acquisition policy at many museums. Much of the field considers the products of Connecticut cabinetmakers to be curiosities rather than highly desirable works of art. Maxim Karolik, for example, collected only furniture made in the prominent port towns such as Salem, Boston, Newport, New York, and Philadelphia. Therefore he left the Museum of Fine Arts a magnificent yet skewed legacy.

Within the past twenty years, a number of studies of Connecticut communities have considered the Connecticut work within the specific context in which it was made and used. While much work has focused on eastern and central Connecticut, particularly New London County and the Connecticut River Valley, less attention has been paid to western Connecticut.[1]

In the third quarter of the eighteenth century, Newtown supported several joiner's shops staffed by native craftsmen who lived and worked according to a conditioned conservatism shared by their fellow townspeople. The artisan's training in Newtown inculcated certain attitudes and provided the particular skills to fulfill the predictable demands of a stable and cohesive population. The native traditionalist joiners did not organize their work to distinguish themselves from other shops or to maximize profits, but rather to satisfy their neighbors. As a result, Newtown furniture tended to be conservative in style, well-finished, and well-constructed.[2]

This particular high chest was made by the leading shop in Newtown in the third quarter of the eighteenth century. While most of the surviving high chests and dressing tables made by this shop are rather plain, this example demonstrates what the joiner could accomplish given the greater desires or purchasing power of a client. The crisply carved ball-and-claw feet, the scrolls behind the knees, and the chamfered front edges of the carcass reveal a close connection to English Georgian traditions of the 1730s and reflect a high degree of skill. The proportions of the high chest and the use of wooden pins to attach

moldings and drawer supports manifest the influence of Low Country traditions that characterized New York and Long Island cabinetworking in the eighteenth century. The carved sunbursts, unusual finials, and use of cherry suggest the impact of a local aesthetic filter. The result is a distinctive high chest combining fashion and tradition, all executed in a workmanlike manner.
E.S.C.

1. Robert Trent, *Hearts & Crowns* (New Haven, Connecticut: New Haven Colony Historical Society, 1977); Robert Trent, "New London Joined Chairs, 1720-1790," *Connecticut Historical Society Bulletin* 50, no. 4 (Fall 1985), pp. 1-195; and William Hosley, Jr. and Gerald W.R. Ward, eds., *The Great River: Art & Society of the Connecticut Valley, 1635-1820* (Hartford: Wadsworth Atheneum, 1985), esp. pp. 185-271.

2. For more information on Newtown and its cabinetmakers, see Edward S. Cooke, Jr., "Rural Artisanal Culture: The Preindustrial Joiners of Newtown and Woodbury, Connecticut, 1760-1820," (Ph.D. diss., Boston University, 1984).

11.

Work Table (**43**)
Boston, Massachusetts, 1795-1805
Mahogany, thuya burl veneer, birch veneer,
rosewood and holly inlay; new bag
H. 28 in., W. 19⅝ in., D. 15⅜ in.

Bequest of Priscilla G. Hall 1990.172

Ladies' work tables of the Federal period reflected the increasingly defined domestic
sphere for women of the new republic. As
changes in transportation, manufacturing,
and trade separated work from home, women
of well-to-do families found their roles more
circumscribed and centered in the home.[1]
With the advent of the ideal of domesticity,
social activities took on greater importance
and specialized furniture for such rituals became necessary. The work table consistently
featured a hanging bag or receptacle for sewing scraps as well as smaller drawers above
for sewing equipment. Options included a
writing surface, compartments in the upper
drawer, and boards for such games as check-
ers or backgammon.[2]

The upper drawer of this particular table
originally had a nicely fitted adjustable writing surface and adjacent storage compartments for ink, sand, and writing implements.
The work bag hangs from a frame that slides
to the side of the table. Finished on all four
sides and set upon casters, the table was
meant to be seen in the round as an important
piece of movable furniture. The best Boston-
area work tables have similar elements. The
decoration further reinforces the Boston ori-
gin: the reeded tapered leg and turned vocabulary of the top – reel, baluster, and four
rings – is found on many Boston work-and-
card tables, and the lunette banding around
the edge of the top is a popular decorative element on many Boston tables and case pieces.
In the past such features were considered the
signature of the preeminent Boston federal
cabinetmakers John and Thomas Seymour,
but recent research has demonstrated that
such features appear on the work of several
shops and that the cabinetmaking trade had a
series of specialists who provided turned legs
or inlay.[3] Although this particular table was
not necessarily made in the Seymour shop, the
thin mahogany drawer linings and Greek key
border around the thuya veneer top – seen
only on the Derby console tables (no. 44) –

suggests that this is a top-of-the-line work table, made by one of the leading shops.
E.S.C.

1. On the social changes during this period, see
Nancy Cott, *The Bonds of Womanhood* (New Haven: Yale University Press, 1977).

2. Charles Montgomery, *American Furniture: The
Federal Period* (New York: The Viking Press, 1966),
pp. 397-422.

3. For the older view, see Vernon Stoneman, *John
and Thomas Seymour, Cabinetmakers in Boston,
1794-1816* (Boston: Special Publications, 1959);
and Stoneman, *A Supplement to John and Thomas
Seymour, Cabinetmakers in Boston, 1794-1816*
(Boston: Special Publications, 1965). This work table is illustrated on p. 74 of the latter. More recent
research on the workings of the Boston furniture
trade can be found in *The Work of Many Hands:
Card Tables in Federal America, 1790-1820* (New
Haven: Yale University Art Gallery, 1982).

12.

Pier Table (one of a pair) (exh. no. 44)
Boston or Salem, 1800-1810
Mahogany, mahogany veneer, burl, rosewood
veneer, birch, white pine, yellow poplar and
brass
H. 35 in., w. 55½ in., D. 24 in.

Gift of Richard Edwards 1972.429

Wealthy merchants in such colonial New England seaports as Salem and Boston were able to patronize the finest craftsmen. Elias Hasket Derby, one of the most prosperous eighteenth-century merchants, purchased furniture by John and Thomas Seymour, had a house designed by Charles Bulfinch, and imported vast quantities of English silver, glass, and ceramics. His daughter Elizabeth, who married Nathaniel West, lived in a magnificent country home called Oak Hill, built between 1800 and 1801 in Danvers, Massachusetts.

The Museum has been fortunate to acquire a number of pieces with documented ownership at Oak Hill, including woodwork from three rooms.[1] Generous gifts from Derby descendents, beginning with Martha Codman's gift in 1923, have facilitated the installation of these three rooms with appropriate family furnishings.[2] In 1972, a gift by Richard Edwards of more than two hundred pieces of Derby-West furniture, Chinese and English porcelain, ceramics, and American glass and silver, inspired a redesigning and refurbishing of the room installations to most accurately accommodate all the gifts received since 1923.

The outstanding objects in Edwards's 1972 gift are a pair of pier tables. Rare in form and decoration, the tables have exceptionally fine carving on the legs and along the top edge, and detailed Greek fret inlay and veneer on the top surface epitomizing the highest level of Anglo-neoclassical style in Boston. The form is derived from a plate in Thomas Sheraton's *Cabinet Directory* (London, 1803) which includes the lower shelf and its brass border. However, the carved and inlayed top is substituted for a marble top which Sheraton recommended.[3] This exceptional decoration suited the table for prominent display in the pier space between two windows.

R.J.M.

1. For a full discussion of the acquisition and installation of Derby-West furnishings and Oak Hill architecture, see the *Museum of Fine Arts, Boston Bulletin*, vol. 81, 1983, with essays by Jonathan Fairbanks, Wendy A. Cooper and Wendy Kaplan.

2. Gifts of Derby-West furnishings were received in the 1920s, 30s and 1940s from Martha Codman, Martha (Codman) and Maxim Karolik, S. Richard Fuller in memory of his wife Lucy Derby (great-granddaughter of Elias Hasket Derby), Mrs. William C. West, and Mrs. David R. McIlwaine in memory of her mother, Margaret Lander Pierce.

3. Cooper, Wendy A. "The Furniture and Furnishings of the Farm at Danvers" *Museum of Fine Arts, Boston Bulletin*, vol. 81, 1983, pp. 24-45.

Adam Hains
(1768-after 1820)

Upholstery attributed to George
Bertault
(working 1793)

13.
Armchair (one of a pair) (exh. no. 45)
Philadelphia, Pennsylvania, about 1792-1797
Mahogany; original upholstery foundation
with modern cover fabric
H. 33 in., W. 23 in., D. 19 in.

Paper label inside rear seat rail: ALL / KINDS
OF /CABINET AND CHAIRWORK / DONE BY /
ADAM HAINS / NO. 135. NORTH THIRD-STREET
/ PHILADELPHIA
Otis Norcross Fund, William Francis Warden
Fund, Gift of a Friend of the Department
1979.486

This exceptional pair of armchairs by Philadelphia cabinetmaker Adam Hains documents the vogue in both Britain and America
for the Louis XVI style in the decades following the American Revolution. This trend can
be ascribed in part to the taste of American
statesmen and merchants living in France
who returned to the new republic with furnishings purchased during their stay abroad.
After ten years in Paris, John Adams returned
to his home in Quincy, Massachusetts, with
French decorations for his home. On a much
larger scale, Boston merchant James Swan
purchased and shipped to the United States
royal furniture confiscated during the French
revolution.[1] It is ironic to note that in spite of
their democratic ideals, post-Revolutionary
Americans felt a special affinity for the splendor
of the *ancien régime.*

The prototype for these particular chairs
may be a French *fauteuil* in the same style
owned by George Washington and now at
Mount Vernon.[2] While the exact design
source for the Museum's chair remains unknown, this example illustrates how local
cabinetmakers probably used imported furniture to enlarge existing French sets and create
adaptations for the American market.

Significantly, the chairs have survived with
their original upholstery foundations. This
material evidence proves that the rigid front
seat edge referred to in the period as a
"French" edge was produced in this country

in the 1790s. The upholsterer for the Museum's chairs may be George Bertault, who
worked in Philadelphia in 1793 and advertised himself as an "upholsterer from Paris."
A surviving 1793 bill paid by Andrew Craigie
of Cambridge, Massachusetts, names Bertault
for the purchase of twelve arm chairs similar
to those in the Museum's collections.[3] The
Haines-labeled Museum chairs and the
Craigie examples enable us to reconsider the
relationship between eighteenth-century up-
holsterers and cabinetmakers. At a time when
the upholstery profession was comparable to
that of a decorator or designer and was held
in higher regard than mere chairmaking,
Bertault could have arranged the sale of the
chairs to Craigie, or the unknown owner of
the Museum's examples, and employed Hains
to construct the chairs.
J.J.F.

1. See Cecilia Jackson Otto, "French Furniture for
American Patriots," *Antiques* 79, no. 4 (April
1961), pp. 370-73, which includes a list of articles
which relate to French furniture brought to America

during this period. For citations on Swan's
purchases, see Jeffrey Munger, "French Upholstery
Practices of the 18th Century" in Edward S. Cooke,
Jr., ed., *Upholstery in America and Europe from the
Seventeenth Century to World War I* (New York:
W.W. Norton & Co. 1987), p. 130, fn. 16, 18.

2. Andrew Passieri and Robert F. Trent "Some
Amazing Washington Chairs, Or, White-and-Gold
Paint and the Square Stitched Edge," *Maine Antiques Digest*, (May 1983), 1C-3C. The Mount
Vernon "fauteuil" may be the same "French chair
for a model" purchased by Washington, presumably
to be copied by local cabinetmakers.

3. The Craigie chairs are in the collection of the
Longfellow National Historic Site, National Park
Service. A related set is at the Vale in Waltham, So-
ciety for the Preservation of New England Antiqui-
ties. A fine summation of these chairs and record of
Craigie's bills are found in Kathleen Catalano and
Richard C. Nylander, "New attributions to Adam
Hains, Philadelphia furniture maker," *Antiques*
117, no. 5 (May 1980) pp. 1112-16. For a pioneer-
ing article on Hains, see Carl M. Williams, "Adam
Hains of Philadelphia, Master Cabinetmaker of the
Marlborough School," *Antiques*, 51, no. 5, (May
1947) pp. 316-17.

14.

Side Chair (exh. no. 49)
Baltimore, Maryland, 1815-1825
Wood, cane, painted decoration
H. 31⅞ in., W. 20⅛ in., D. 21 in.

Gift of Jean and Michael Dingman and Otis
Norcross Fund 1981.26

The neoclassical style in art, architecture, and
dress reflected the American identification
with Greek and Roman civilization following
the establishment of the federal government
in 1789. In Baltimore, neoclassicism flour-
ished well into the early nineteenth century.
The city had prospered as a trade center during the Revolutionary War, and grew dramatically between 1790 and 1810. During the
same period, the number of cabinetmakers increased from two to eighty to meet the growing demand for furniture.[1] Increased production in turn fostered such specialists as
turners, carvers, caners, and painters. This
last specialty was in great demand following
the immigration of English-trained painters
and the introduction of painted furniture to
Baltimore in the 1780s and 1790s. Paint decoration could include scenes of local Baltimore architecture or fanciful motifs derived
from contemporary illustrations. This particular chair's crest rail is decorated with an image of griffins similar to that on a plate titled
"Ornament for a Frieze or Tablet" in Thomas
Sheraton's *The Cabinetmaker and Upholsterer's Drawing Book*, first printed in
London in 1793 and again in 1803. Other
Sheraton motifs include the painted bellflow-
ers and lines on the front turned legs, intended to imitate inlay and stringing commonly used on early neoclassical chairs.
However, the concave curves of the klismos
chair and the painted classical urn and anthe-
mion decoration indicate it was made in the
later more archeologically accurate styled
neoclassicism. This allusion to the classical
era ideally suited this chair, part of a set of
nineteen pieces of furniture, for Mondawmin,
the Greek revival residence into which noted
Baltimore banker Alexander Brown moved in
the 1830s.[2]

R.J.M.

1. Gregory R. Weidman, *Furniture in Maryland
1740-1940* (Baltimore: Maryland Historical Society, 1984), p. 71.

2. William Voss Elder, III, *Baltimore Painted Furniture, 1800-1840* (Baltimore: Baltimore Museum of
Art, 1972), p. 61.

Attributed to John Finlay
(1777-1851) or

Hugh Finlay
(1781-1831)

15. (color plate)
Grecian Couch (exh. no. 53)
Baltimore, Maryland, 1820-1840
Yellow poplar, cherry, white pine; rosewood
graining and gilded painting; partial original
foundation and new foundation materials,
cover, and trim
H. 35¾ in., W. 91½ in., D. 24¼ in.

Gift of Mr. and Mrs. Amos B. Hostetter, Jr.,
Anne and Joseph P. Pellegrino, Mr. and Mrs.
Peter S. Lynch, Mr. William N. Banks, Jr.,
Eddy G. Nicholson, Mr. and Mrs. John Las-
tavica, Mr. and Mrs. Daniel F. Morley, and
Mary S. and Edward J. Holmes Fund
1988.530

In the early nineteenth century, Baltimore was the fastest growing city in the new nation. Its commercial vitality – it exported grain and other agricultural products from the Chesapeake Bay and Susquehanna Valley, and supported light manufacturing in town – fostered demand for household furnishings of the latest fashion and attracted talented craftsmen and artists. The architects Benjamin H. Latrobe and Robert Mills played a particularly important role in establishing a high-quality built environment. The classical, archaeologically derived designs of these architects were executed by local craftsmen, many of whom were recent immigrants from England.[1]

Painted Baltimore furniture made in the second quarter of the nineteenth century has received considerable attention and acclaim as the most aesthetically rich and appealing furniture of that period. The combination of robust, archaeologically inspired forms and gilt-painted classical decoration endowed this furniture with a strong cosmopolitan presence. The leading painters working in Baltimore during this period were the Finlay brothers, Irish-trained craftsmen who worked together and independently during this period. In 1809 the Finlays painted a lavish suite of furniture designed by Latrobe for the Madison White House. Much of their work from the first two decades of the century featured single ground colors with gilt striped

legs and panels with floral, landscape, or armorial motifs. Their later work of the 1820s and 1830s demonstrates a surer, more painterly manner in which gilt classical anthemia, rosettes, and acanthus leaves decorated grained surfaces. Several examples of the Finlays' work of this period survive in Baltimore museums.

When the Museum acquired this couch in 1988, it was one of the rare Finlay examples not already in a public institution. Its frame construction and painted decoration link it to sets of furniture made by the Finlays for the Wilson and Ridgely families and to a couch currently in the Kaufmann collection. Although this particular couch has a yellow poplar frame rather than a walnut one, the elaborate casters and thread evidence of the original crimson silk cover identify this couch as one of the most stylish of its sort. Originally finished with tinted varnish to imitate the effect of fire gilding, the decorative casters complement the free-hand gilding on the frame.[2] According to estate inventories and auction catalogs, crimson was the most popular fabric color for Baltimore furniture in the classical style, followed by orange or yellow. Silk damask fabric was found in the best parlors, while moreen was used in other parlors and dining rooms. This couch retains its origi-

nal foundation at the head and the original edge roll along the front and has been recovered with a reproduction crimson silk documented to the period and basing the pillows, bolster, and trimming on contemporary sources. The quality of the materials and the paucity of padding indicate that the Grecian couch, referred to in period documents as a "fancy Lounge," was more of a social statement than a comfortable couch in which one could relax.[3]

E.S.C.

1. Gregory Weidman, *Furniture in Maryland, 1740-1940* (Baltimore: The Maryland Historical Society, 1984), pp. 70-95.

2. I am indebted to Christine Thomson, furniture conservator for the Society for the Preservation of New England Antiquities, for her analysis of the casters.

3. On the related examples, see J. Michael Flanigan, *American Furniture from the Kaufmann Collection* (Washington: National Gallery of Art, 1986), pp. 156-157. For information on Baltimore fabric preferences, see letter to the author from Gregory Weidman, February 15, 1989 (letter in data file, Department of American Decorative Arts and Sculpture, Museum of Fine Arts, Boston); and catalogue of the auction of the estate of William Taylor, May 22, 1838 (Maryland Historical Society, Baltimore).

16.

Center Table (exh. no. 60)
Possibly New York, New York, about 1850
Rosewood and rosewood veneer; new marble
top
H. 30 in., DIAM. 37 in.

Edwin E. Jack Fund 1981.402

As the focal point of the nineteenth-century
American parlor, the center table provided
the visitor with a selection of prized family
possessions including Bibles and photograph
albums. Center tables also reflected the
owner's awareness of the latest fashions, such
as the Gothic revival style, which became
popular in America by mid-century.

The first "gothick" ornament on American
furniture was inspired by eighteenth-century
English cabinetmaker's guides, such as those
produced by Thomas Chippendale.[1] Toward
the end of the century a romantic gothic sensibility was first expressed in the novels of
Philadelphian Charles Brockton Brown and
the buildings of architects Maximillian
Godefroy and Benjamin Henry Latrobe. By
1837, publications by English architect A.W.
Pugin championing the more archaeologically
correct designs for domestic and ecclesiastical
Gothic had propelled the style into international prominence. Pugin's exhortation that
all decoration must enrich an essential element of a structure and serve a purpose car-
ried a moral message that inspired American
architects and furnituremakers. Pugin can be
directly credited with the flowering of the
style at mid-century.[2]

The finest examples of American Gothic revival architecture and furnishings are found in
Tarrytown, New York, at Lyndhurst, designed
by Alexander Jackson Davis in 1838. However, it was Andrew Jackson Downing's 1850
publication of *The Architecture of Country
Houses* that popularized the style. Downing's
book contained numerous examples of houses
and furniture from the humblest cottage to
elaborate villas, and inspired craftsmen-build-
ers and cabinetmakers. One of his illustrations may have served as the design source for
the maker or designer of this table.[3]

Like most Gothic revival furniture, the
center table romantically evokes the medieval
past rather than authentically duplicating a
work of the period. The cluster column legs
resemble the pillars found in medieval

churches, while the pointed arches and trefoil
decoration are essentials of the Gothic vocabulary as seen through nineteenth-century
eyes.[4] Despite the popularity of the style, few
examples as fine as this center table survive.
J.J.F.

1. Thomas Chippendale, *The Gentleman and Cabi-
net-maker's Director* (London: Printed for the author, 1762), plates 16, 17, 25. An excellent analysis
of the literary and visual sources of the Gothic revival is in Alice P. Kenney and Leslie J. Workman,
"Ruins, Romance, and Reality, Medievalism in An-
glo-American Imagination and Taste, 1750-1840,"
Winterthur Portfolio 10 (1975) 131-63.

2. Two of Augustus Welby Pugin's best-known
works are *Contrasts, or a Parallel between the No-
ble Edifices of the Middle Ages and Corresponding
Buildings of the Present Day Shewing the Present
Decay of Taste* (London: printed for the author,
1836), and *The True Principles of Pointed or Christian Architecture* (London: J. Weale, 1841).

3. *Lyndhurst, On the Hudson River, Tarrytown,
N.Y.* (Washington, D.C.: National Trust for Historic Preservation, 1973). Andrew Jackson Downing, *The Architecture of Country Houses: Including
Designs for Cottages, and Farm-Houses, and Villas,
with Remarks on Interiors, Furniture, and the Best
Modes of Warming and Ventilating.* (New York: D.
Appleton and Co., 1850). Reprint. New York: Dover Publications, Inc., figure 179.

4. For a survey of Gothic imagery in America, see
Katherine S. Howe and David B. Warren, *The
Gothic Revival Style in America, 1830-1870* (Hous-
ton: The Museum of Fine Arts, Houston, 1976).
For a related table attributed to A. J. Davis, see exh.
no. 73.

Ignatius Lutz
(active 1844-1860)

17.
Sideboard (exh. no. 62)
Philadelphia, Pennsylvania, 1850-1860
Oak, yellow poplar; marble
H. 94 in., W. 74 in., D. 25 in.

Stenciled label on back of lower section:
"FROM / I. LUTZ' / CABINET WAREHOUSE / No.
121 S. 11th St. / PHIL"
Gift of the Estate of Richard Bruce E. Lacont
1990.1

Sideboards with elaborately carved fish, fowl, vegetables, and fruit are an archetypal mid-nineteenth-century American furniture form. At the international exhibitions of the period, furniture firms chose to display sideboards to demonstrate their sophisticated sense of design and execution. The Parisian firm of Alexandre Georges Fourdinois exhibited at the 1851 Crystal Palace show a monumental example that was very architectonic in massing with Renaissance revival features, elaborate moldings and rich carving. In America, French- and German-trained cabinetmakers who migrated in the middle of the century produced simpler sideboards in which certain Renaissance features such as the caryatids and consoles were eliminated, but the naturalistic carving and large mass were retained. Prominently placed in dining rooms and often laden with silver, the sideboards gave material definition to the importance of social rituals involved in eating.[1]

Philadelphia supported a furniture industry of small shops staffed by well-trained immigrant cabinetmakers who relied upon handwork rather than machine power. One of the largest of these was owned by Ignatius Lutz, who came to Philadelphia from France in 1844. Lutz was the proprietor of a shop with thirty craftsmen who worked without power machinery.[2] His sideboard is quite extraordinary in its material, shape, and vitality. In contrast to the walnut examples with very rectilinear massing typical of such prominent cabinetmakers as Alexander Roux, Lutz used oak and combined pleasingly swelled components to build the overall mass. The expressive quality of the naturalistic carving also attests to Lutz's skill and makes the sideboard a dramatic tour-de-force of Victorian America.
E.S.C.

1. Kenneth Ames, "The Battle of the Sideboards," *Winterthur Portfolio* 9 (1974), pp. 1-27; and Gerald W.R. Ward, *American Case Furniture in the Mabel Brady Garvan and Other Collections at Yale University* (New Haven: Yale University Art Gallery, 1988), pp. 431-434.

2. Ignatius Lutz Declaration of Intention (August 26, 1844) and Oath of Allegiance (May 10, 1850), Pennsylvania Supreme Court Records, Pennsylvania Division of Archives and Manuscripts, Harrisburg, Pennsylvania; Philadelphia Social History Project, University of Pennsylvania, "1850 Census of Manufactures" and "1860 Census of Manufactures," (computerized format on deposit at the Van Pelt Library at the University of Pennsylvania); and Charles Venable, "Philadelphia Biedermeier: Germanic Craftsmen and Design in Philadelphia, 1820-1850" (M.A. thesis, University of Delaware, 1986).

Herter Brothers
(1865-1905)

18.
Side Chair (exh. no. 65)
New York, New York, about 1880
Cherry, light wood marquetry; ebonized finish and gilded detailing; original upholstery foundation, new cover fabric and trim
H. 34¼ in., w. 17 in., D. 18¼ in.

Gift of the Estate of Richard Bruce E. Lacont
1990.105

In the third quarter of the nineteenth century the excesses of contemporary revival styles led artists, architects, and other visual artists to create a style based upon elemental or minimalist structure with Gothic or Japanese elements for decoration. In England the leading designer of the new "Art Furniture" was E.W. Godwin, while in America it was the furniture and decorating firm Herter Brothers.[1]

Gustave Herter (1830-1898) and his half-brother Christian (1840-1883) were typical of the new designers who worked for the most fashionable firms. The former had studied in Paris, worked for an architect, and then emigrated to America, working first as a silver designer for the predecessors of Tiffany & Co.; the latter studied at the Ecole des Beaux-Arts and later studied painting with Pierre Victor Galland. Like Tiffany & Co., Herter Brothers hired a variety of designers, many of whom had architectural or artistic training abroad, and depended upon skilled immigrants to execute the elaborate work. The firm collaborated on furniture or entire interiors with such architects as McKim, Mead, and White or Richard Morris Hunt and counted among its clients such wealthy industrialists as Jay Gould, J. Pierpont Morgan, James T. Goodwin, William Henry Vanderbilt, Collis Huntington, Mark Hopkins, and Darius Ogden Mills. These commissions indicate that the firm made furniture in a variety of styles – Rococo, Renaissance, Gothic, or Queen Anne – but its most distinctive work was its Anglo-Japanese furniture.[2]

While not branded with the Herter stamp (few of their pieces were), this chair features a stamped number – 3631 – and a pencil inscription "Store." The inscription and stamped number link it to a pair of identical chairs, one owned by the Cleveland Museum

of Art and one by the Yale University Art Gallery, that were part of a set made by Herter Brothers for Mark Hopkins. Chairs of identical shape but in rosewood were also made for James Goodwin and accompanied a stamped table. Such relationships with documented Herter sets provide a strong attribution for this chair.[3] The form itself draws from the ebonized work of such English designers as Godwin and Bruce Talbert, but is handled in a manner that is fresh and new, one that combines the Japanese inlaid motifs of the crest rail and the Chinese architectural lattice of the back. The resulting chair blends eastern-influenced motifs with high-style western art furniture details.

E.S.C.

1. For a recent summary of this period, see Elizabeth Aslin, *E. W. Godwin: Furniture and Interior Decoration* (London: John Murray, 1986).

2. Marilynn Johnson, "Art Furniture: Wedding the Beautiful to the Useful," in *In Pursuit of Beauty: Americans and the Aesthetic Movement* (New York: The Metropolitan Museum of Art and Rizzoli, 1986), pp. 143-175; Catherine Hoover Voorsanger, "Dictionary of Architects, Artists, and Manufacturers," in *Ibid.*, pp. 438-440; and Wendy Kaplan, ed., *"The Art that is Life": The Arts & Crafts Movement in America, 1875-1920* (Boston: Museum of Fine Arts, Boston, 1987), esp. p. 72.

3. For a discussion of the Hopkins chairs, see Henry Hawley, "An 'Aesthetic' Sidechair," *The Bulletin of The Cleveland Museum of Art* 69, no. 12 (December 1982), pp. 330-332.

S. Karpen & Bros.

19.
Armchair (exh. no. 69)
Chicago, Illinois, 1901-1910
Mahogany, maple; gold leaf; original foundation and final cover with some new final cover on the seat, back, and arms
H. 42 in., W. 32½ in., D. 25½ in.
Gift of Daniel and Jesse Lie Farber 1986.749

At the Paris Exposition of 1900, a group of French designers and craftsmen introduced a new style, Art Nouveau, derived from the organicism of nature rather than the rectilinearity of historic fashion. The style was characterized by bulging forms, curling whiplash tendrils, and floral imagery. Although the style had an immediate impact on American ceramics and metals, it exerted little influence on American furniture. In Chicago two firms offered a small line of Art Nouveau furniture, the Tobey Furniture Company and S. Karpen & Bros.[1]

S. Karpen & Bros. specialized in upholstered parlor furniture for the medium to high end of the market. Very aggressive in its marketing, the firm advertised that it offered the "most expensive and daring designs ever attempted in carved furniture in America." Constantly adapting to the market, the firm developed lines in a number of styles ranging from colonial revival to overstuffed Renaissance revival to austere Mission. Karpen & Bros. introduced the Art Nouveau style in 1901 and featured it in a display at the 1904 Saint Louis World's Fair, where it received the Grand Prize for upholstered furniture. To maximize flexibility and simplify the manufacturing process, the company used the latest technology. Doweled frames eliminated time-consuming cutting of joints, spindle carving machines roughed out as many as eight duplicate pieces, and tufting machines eliminated time-consuming finish upholstery. These processes and machines enabled Karpen & Bros. to offer fashionable work to the middle class. For high-end work, the firm added more adventurous designs, more handwork, and better grades of fabric.[2]

This armchair is a muscular version of the rare American Art Nouveau style. The female figure on the crest rail resembles the American dancer Loie Fuller (1862-1928), who per-

formed a dance at the 1900 Exposition that shared the motion of the Art Nouveau style. Dressed in flowing silks and using theatrical lighting, Fuller moved like a butterfly or became a lilly. The design for the chair was originally modelled in clay by a sculptor working for Karpen & Bros. A plaster cast of this model served as the guide for the spindle shapers on the multiple carving machines. A group of skilled carvers then finished and refined the carving on the set of chairs produced by the machines. Chairs were available either in finished or gilded mahogany. The gilding, largely original silk cover, and hand tufting of this example indicates that it was intended for the high end of the market. Yet the wire webbing and wire edge of the upholstery foundation demonstrate that the firm relied upon

modern technology rather than on traditional craft practices for the fabrication of the basic chair.[3]

E.S.C.

1. Gabriel Weisberg, *Art Nouveau Bing: Paris Style 1900* (New York: Abrams, 1986); and Sharon Darling, *Chicago Furniture: Art, Craft, & Industry, 1833-1983* (New York: W.W. Norton, 1984), pp. 194-196.
2. Darling, pp. 70-74.
3. Darling, pp. 195-196.

20.

Buffet (exh. no. 74)
Vincennes, Indiana, about 1800
Yellow poplar, curly maple
H. 46¼ in., W. 48 in., D. 24¼ in.

Gift of Daniel and Jesse Lie Farber and Frank
B. Bemis Fund 1989.50

Museum collections of American furniture have highlighted the Anglo and Germanic traditions of the East Coast, overlooking the thriving French culture of the Mississippi Valley, particularly the upper Mississippi Valley area known at the time as the Illinois country.[1] In the last half of the eighteenth century, Vincennes, Indiana, was an active fur trade center closely connected with Detroit to the north and Saint Louis and Kaskaskia to the west. Most of its population had roots in French-Canada, and local merchants would usually hire boatmen and engagés, or indentured servants, from that area. During the 1760s French troops withdrew, the Jesuits were suppressed, and more Anglos immigrated from the coastal colonies, but Vincennes retained much of its French character.[2]

A buffet from Vincennes clearly demonstrates the conscious retention of Creole culture and a rejection of the encroaching Anglo culture. Used to store dishes, utensils, and food, the buffet was a French form that served the same purpose as the Anglo sideboard or huntboard. Unlike the French-Canadian furniture in Quebec and Creole furniture in New Orleans during this period – much of which was characterized by such Anglo features as inlaid patera, imported English brasses, and veneered surfaces – the buffet is clearly the product of a small, local shop, isolated from English influence. The panelled construction, curved skirt and moldings, asymmetrical door panels, hand-forged fische hinges, and drawer construction (single large tails join the drawer sides to the fronts and backs, and the bottom rests in grooves on all four sides) link this example to French provincial work in the Louis XV style. The specific shape of the foot, the central sunburst carved on the skirt, the carved floral returns on the door panels, the gouge-carved scale decoration on the stiles, the drawer configuration, and abstracted egg-and-dart molding along the edges of the drawers are typical of work made in the Manche area of Normandy. In France, such buffets were usually made of cherry with thick oak drawer linings. French-Canadian examples are often of yellow birch with thick pine linings. In contrast, the Vincennes buffet has thin yellow poplar drawer linings and a yellow poplar and curly maple carcass and curly maple top, all of which was colored with red ocher (iron oxide) paint streaked with a darker pigment. The survival of the original

finish is extremely rare, for many examples have been stripped in the twentieth century.[3]

The inside of the buffet provides clues about its origins. A new shelf, apparently added in the mid-nineteenth century to replace the original, bears the inscription "From: Sisters of Providence / St. Marys, Vigo Co." The writing refers to St. Mary's of the Woods, a convent founded in Terre Haute in 1828, where the buffet was owned until the 1920s. A history in the Wabash valley and local woods suggest that the buffet was made in the area's major town of Vincennes, probably by an engagé who learned joinery in the Manche tradition either in Normandy or in Canada. Two cabinetmakers are known to have worked in Vincennes: Pierre Roux and Pierre Antoine Petit dit Lalumiere. Roux trained in Geneva, Switzerland, and made cherry wardrobes in a different French style. Lalumiere is a possible maker for this buffet. Two of his daughters attended St. Mary's of the Woods in Terre Haute.[4]
E.S.C.

1. Francis J. Puig, "The Early Furniture of the Mississippi River Valley, 1760-1820," in Francis J. Puig and Michael Conforti, eds., *The American Craftsman and the European Tradition, 1620-1820* (Minneapolis: The Minneapolis Institute of Arts, 1989), pp. 152-178.

2. Gilbert Imlay, *A Topographical Description of the Western Territory of North America* (London, 1797; reprint ed. New York: Johnson Reprint Corporation, 1968), esp. 496-499; C. F. Volney, *A View of the Soil and Climate of the United States of America* (Philadelphia, 1804; reprint ed. New York: Hafner Publishing Co., 1968), pp. 331-351; and Carl Ekberg and William Foley, eds., *An Account of Upper Louisiana* (Columbia, Missouri: University of Missouri Press, 1989).

3. Jean Palardy, *The Early Furniture of French Canada* (Toronto: Macmillan, 1963); and Suzanne Tardieu-Dumont, *Le mobilier regional francais – Normandie* (Paris: Berger-Levrault, 1980), pp. 10, 20, 114, and 119.

4. Author's conversations with Douglas Solliday of Columbia, Missouri, February, 1989; and with Richard Day of Vincennes, Indiana, March, 1989.

Heinrich Kuenemann II
(1843-1914)

21.
Wardrobe (exh. no. 75)
Fredericksburg, Texas, about 1870
Pine
H. 87¼ in., W. 56½ in., D. 23½ in.

Gift of Mrs. Charles L. Bybee 1990.483

In extending the temporal, regional, and ethnic basis of its collection, the Department of American Decorative Arts and Sculpture has been fortunate to have the support and interest of such individuals as Faith Bybee, a Texan who has devoted her life to preserving and collecting pioneer Texas-German material. Beginning in the early 1820s, declining economic opportunities in Germany prompted a large emigration to America. The earliest settled Texas-German area was between the lower Brazos and Colorado Rivers, but in 1845 the Society for the Protection of German Immigrants in Texas began to establish communities in the western hill country. Fredericksburg and New Braunfels became the centers of this German region and each supported about ten cabinetmakers' shops in the 1860s. Most of these craftsmen produced furniture in the Biedermeier styles then popular in their home country. Serving a population that was itself 85 percent German, German joiners in small shops dominated the trade until the 1870s, when factory-made furniture began to encroach upon their monopoly.[1]

This particular wardrobe, called a kleiderschrank in contemporary documents, illustrates well the interface of traditional ethnic notions of fashion and cosmopolitan popular notions. The wardrobe remained a favored expensive storage form in many German-settled areas of the United States, and Germanic cabinetmakers in Texas apparently built many. The wardrobes of the Fredericksburg cabinetmakers Johann Peter Tatsch and Heinrich Kuenemann II are particularly successful examples. The work is very architectural with moldings separating base from midsection from capital. The heavy mortise-and-tenoned construction, beveled panels, scalloped skirt with vestigial center foot, and simple Biedermeier cornice of this wardrobe link it to native conventions, yet Kuenemann adapted it to local materials. Eschewing black walnut, which was available, he used the curly pine of the area to provide visual focal points on the panels and less-figured pine for the framing members. The pine of these framing members was probably originally darkened with a copal varnish. Like his father-in-law Tatsch, Kuenemann incorporated aspects of factory furniture during the 1870s. The applied rondel on the frieze, the composition

lock escutcheons, the spiral-turned colonettes, and wooden drawer pulls may even have been stock items imported to Fredericksburg. Even the great size of the moldings at the edge of the rails and stiles and the use of screws to secure the panels indicates that Kuenemann internalized construction features of the mass market. His blending of tradition, local materials, and popular style demonstrates how Texan-Germans adapted their material culture to external force during a very dynamic period.[2]

E.S.C.

1. Lonn Taylor and David Warren, *Texas Furniture: The Cabinetmakers and Their Work, 1840-1880* (Austin: University of Texas Press, 1975), pp. 6-7 and 30-37.

2. On the popularity of wardrobes in German-American culture, see Scott Swank et al, *Arts of the Pennsylvania Germans* (New York: W.W. Norton, 1983), pp. 50-51 and 160-166; Charles van Ravenswaay, *The Arts and Architecture of German Settlements in Missouri* (Columbia: University of Missouri Press, 1977), pp. 354-366; and Taylor and Warren, pp. 69-110. Wardrobes by Tatsch are illustrated and discussed in Taylor and Warren, pp. 98-101. For information on Kuenemann, I am grateful for the help of Nina Nixon-Mendez, director of the Gillespie County Historical Society, and her staff.

Charles Eames
(1907-1978)

22.
Side Chair, Model DCW (exh. no. 90)
Venice, California, 1946
Walnut plywood, rubber, metal
H. 28¾ in., w. 19¼ in., D. 20½ in.

Label: Herman Miller (logo)/ Evans (logo)/
Charles Eames
Gift of Edward J. Wormley 1975.31

Twentieth-century furniture design has been influenced by, and in turn has influenced the development of new materials and manufacturing processes. Improved methods of steel production, metal plating, and welding in the early twentieth century fostered new furniture construction. Marcel Breuer designed the first modern chair to incorporate tubular steel in 1925, and tubular steel became the most popular modern furniture medium throughout the twenties and thirties.[1] In the thirties designers such as Alvar Aalto combined metal and laminated plywood to form chairs, but aesthetics were sometimes compromised in the quest for the ideal composition. In the 1940s Charles Eames, collaborating with his wife Ray Kaiser and Eero Saarinen, experimented with a variety of techniques – traditional bent wood, tubular steel, and laminated plywood – to achieve more pleasing forms.

The Eameses had experimented with molded plywood for stretchers, splints and glider shells for the United States Navy during World War II. Unlike Aalto and other designers who had molded plywood in one direction, the Eameses molded the plywood across two planes to create comfortable chair seats and back rests without the need of upholstery. The Museum of Modern Art introduced both the DCW (Dining chair wood) and DCM (Dining chair metal) in a 1946 show entitled "Furniture Designs by Charles Eames." Another new fabrication technique – electronic cycle-welding – was used to fuse rubber shock mounts to the wooden support structure, eliminating evidence of construction from the front of the chair, and allowing for greater structural resiliency.

The DCW model label combines the names of manufacturers Herman Miller and Evans,

indicating a date of manufacture around 1946, when Evans produced the chair parts, and Herman Miller first began assembling and distributing the finished product. After 1948, Herman Miller possessed sole rights to manufacture and distribute the Eames chair.[2] By the early 1950s the DCW model was discontinued. The tubular metal supports of the DCM design were considered more graceful than the wooden supports of the DCW design. The seat and back of the DCW model are composed of a different plywood thickness than the support and legs. This was considered less efficient and less visually pleasing than the clean lines of the metal supports on the DCM model, still in production today.

R.J.M.

1. Christopher Wilk, "Furnishing the Future: Bent Wood and Metal Furniture, 1925-1946" in *Bent Wood and Metal Furniture, 1850-1946*, ed. Derek E. Ostergard (New York: The American Federation of Arts, 1987), pp. 121-174. See also David A. Hanks, *Innovative Furniture in America from 1800 to the Present* (New York: Horizon Press, 1981).

2. Existing labels with just the Evans name suggest the Evans Product Co. of Venice, California originally produced chair prototypes for Eames in 1946. Both the DCM and the DCW chairs now at the Museum were exhibited in the Museum of Modern Art's 1947 exhibition "One hundred useful objects of fine design," following which they were given to the donor, renowned 1950s industrial designer Edward J. Wormley.

Sam Maloof
(b. 1916)

23.
Rocking Chair (exh. no. 100)
Alta Loma, California, 1975
Walnut, ebony
H. 45 in., W. 27¾ in., D. 46 in.

Signed on underside of seat: "MOFA BOSTON /
Sam Maloof 1975 F.A.C.C. / NO. 79"
Purchased through funds provided by the National Endowment for the Arts and The Gillette Corporation 1976.122

In post-World War II America economic prosperity and a growing reaction against cold or poorly made mass-produced furniture transformed the avocational spirit of craft emphasized by the Arts and Crafts movement earlier in the century and inspired some people to undertake careers in the crafts. Liberal-arts majors or industrial designers rather than products of an apprenticeship system, these self-taught woodworkers embraced the personal warmth of wood, enjoyed working the material, and worked in Scandinavian modern or colonial revival styles that evoked high-quality workmanship and more direct relationships between craftsman-designer and client.[1]

Sam Maloof is recognized internationally as the one of the pre-eminent first-generation studio furnituremakers. He turned to furniture in 1948 after working for several years as a graphic and industrial designer. While his basic forms are very straightforward and functional, he devotes considerable attention to sculptural shaping. Not a technical purist, Maloof favors expedient means. He uses bandsaws and disc sanders to rough out stock, routers to cut strong tongue and groove joints where his chair legs meet the seat, and screws and dowels to join parts. Yet he cuts dovetails by hand for his drawers or case furniture because he finds such work more efficient and aesthetically pleasing than using jigged machines. This approach to joinery permits him to spend more time using hand tools like gouges, rasps, and spokeshaves to model the final form. His work is noted for its rich contrasts: soft rounded edges and sharp hard lines can be found on the same arm, scooped out surfaces of a seat contrast with the bulging mass of a crest rail, and exposed decorative joinery, much of which is cut with machines yet shaped with hand tools. Maloof has quietly but consistently refined his early designs, adjusting details, trying different modeling effects, and experimenting with spatial organization of parts. For example, he makes about ten basic chair types but personalizes them in a number of ways: by making an upholstered seat or plank seat, crest rail or spindle back, flat arm

or swooping arm, by using different woods, and of course, different shaping. His work was included in such landmark craft or furniture exhibitions as "Objects USA" (1969), "Woodenworks" (1972), "New Handmade Furniture" (1979), "Poetry of the Physical" (1986), and "The Eloquent Object" (1987). In recognition of his commitment to the furniture and craft fields, Maloof also received a MacArthur Fellowship in 1985. He is the only American craftsperson so honored.[2]

Maloof's most famous piece of furniture is his rocking chair, one of which is in the White House collection. He has made versions in Brazilian rosewood, English brown oak, and maple, but has worked predominantly in black walnut. Elegantly proportioned, comfortable, and shaped to enhance its tactile

qualities, this particular chair was one the first examples of American furniture made by a living craftsman to be accessioned as part of the Museum's "Please Be Seated" program. Funding from the National Endowment for the Arts, matched by a grant from the Gillette Corporation, permitted the Museum to commission public seating for galleries through this nationally acclaimed program.
E.S.C.

1. On the development of American studio furniture, see Edward S. Cooke, Jr., *New American Furniture* (Boston: Museum of Fine Arts, Boston, 1989), esp. pp. 10-31.

2. Maloof has been the subject of numerous articles, but the best source is his autobiography: *Sam Maloof: Woodworker* (New York: Kodansha International, 1983).

James Prestini
(b. 1908)

24.
Bowl (exh. no. 101)
Chicago, Illinois, 1922-1953
Birch
H. 4⅝ in., D. 10½ in.

Marked on bottom: PRESTINI
Gift of James Prestini 1980.394

James Prestini is credited with beginning the modern movement of designer-craftsmen wood turners.[1] After receiving a degree in mechanical engineering at Yale, Prestini taught mathematics at Lake Forest Academy in Illinois where in 1933 he began seriously turning bowls and plates in the school wood-working shop. In 1939, he moved to Chicago and joined the staff at the Institute of Design, founded by former Bauhaus member Laszlo Moholy-Nagy. There Prestini absorbed Bauhaus principles concerning form, design, and materials, subsequently reflected in his turned pieces. Working as a designer and craftsman on the lathe, a machine commonly associated with mass production, Prestini turned blocks of hardwood into common utilitarian forms. For Prestini, the common form combined with the wood's natural grain pattern composed the object's beauty.

Of the twelve turned objects by Prestini in the Museum's collection, there are nine bowls, one platter, one plate and one vase. Prestini preferred common woods to produce these forms – birch, cherry, walnut, satinwood, Cuban and Mexican mahogany. Most of the shapes have a flat, footless bottom, and gradually flaring sides. While later turners as Bob Stocksdale allow the grain of a single piece of wood to determine the size and shape of the finished piece, Prestini often laminated different pieces of wood together to create a larger form.
R.J.M.

1. John Kelsey, "The Turned Bowl," *Fine Woodworking*, January/February, 1982, np.

Bob Stocksdale
(b. 1913)

25.
Bowl (exh. no. 102)
Berkeley, California, 1980
Macadamia wood
H. 3⅜ in., DIAM. (rim) 3¾ in.

Signed: Macadamia/from/California/Bob Stocksdale/1980
Harriet Otis Cruft Fund 1980.389

In the last four decades, lathe-turned vessels have become a sophisticated art form. Bob Stocksdale, who began turning wood at a Conscientious Objecter camp during World War II, refined the craft established by James Prestini from 1922 to 1953.[1] While Prestini's utilitarian forms reflect Bauhaus principles of industrial design, Bob Stocksdale uses such exotic woods as African blackwood, Madagascar rosewood, Los Gatos black walnut, Thai teak, zebrawood, and macadamia wood, and allows the shape and grain of the wood to dictate the ultimate form of the vessel.

Stocksdale turned this bowl on an axis to develop the two "starburst" patterns from the grain's orientation. The graceful curve of the body causes light to play off the grain at different angles, further enhancing the starburst effect.
R.J.M.

1. Richard La Trobe-Bateman, "World-Class Turner," *American Craft* 47, no. 6, December 1987/January 1988, pp. 30-35.

Rude Osolnik
(b. 1915)

26.
Vessel (exh. no. 110)
Berea, Kentucky, 1987
Birch plywood
H. 10¾ in., DIAM. 9⅜ in.

Signed on base: "Osolnik Originals / Laminated birch plywood / '87"
Gift of Daniel and Jesse Lie Farber 1988.234

The Museum's collection of American turned vessels is one of the strongest in the country, ranging from James Prestini's explorations of formal design to Mark Lindquist's sculptural work or Mike Shuler's technical achievements. In turning's transformation from a traditional craft based on vernacular roots to an innovative one committed to experimentation in design and technique, Rude Osolnik has played a major role.[1]

Osolnik began turning in 1927 and, after receiving a M.A. in industrial arts in 1937, accepted a teaching position at Berea College in Kentucky. In addition to teaching, he maintained his own turning shop. Much of his earlier work reflects his training in industrial design and arts. Favoring darker woods like walnut, rosewood, and Macassar ebony, he sought to perfect formal relationships, his most successful and recognizable being his hourglass candlesticks. At the same time, Osolnik's teaching kept his mind open to new ideas, which he explored in one-of-a-kind bowls and vases. In the 1940s he began to use "found wood" rather than perfect blocks from the middle of the tree. He first experimented with spurs, wood from the root area that was considered waste by a nearby veneer mill. The wild grain and rich colors excited Osolnik and forced him to free up his notions of manipulation. In the 1960s, he was one of the first turners to turn vessels from wood with checks and with bark left on the rim. To many contemporaries, such vessels appeared disfigured. But Osolnik was a trailblazer in responding to the individual personalities of a broad range of wood and in highlighting these traits without overpowering them. He took what nature offered and worked within those parameters.

Although Osolnik turned mostly natural woods, he began to experiment with other wood-based materials. In the 1950s he worked with the Office of Economic Opportunity to develop polymer impregnation techniques that would permit utilization of the native oak as long-wearing floorboards. The program was intended to vitalize the local Appalachian lumber industry and provide means for low-cost housing. However, Osolnik used the techniques to make up rough blocks with polymers of different colors and then turned these blocks into vessels. In 1965, he began to laminate Baltic birch plywood together to achieve a powerful graphic form with artificial figure. His use of plywood, that most basic material of rough carpentry, playfully points out the absurdity of the obsession with the perfect block of wood that characterized turning in the 1960s.
E.S.C.

1. Osolnik has only recently gained recognition: *Rude Osolnik: A Retrospective* (Asheville, N.C.: Southern Highland Handicraft Guild, 1990); and Jane Kessler, "Rude Osolnik: By Nature Defined," *American Craft* 50, no. 1 (February/March 1990), pp. 54-57.

Edward Zucca
(b. 1946)

27.
XVIIIth Dynasty Television (exh. no. 111)
Woodstock, Connecticut, 1989
Honduran mahogany, yellow poplar, ebony;
gold leaf, silver leaf, rush; latex paint,
ebonizing
H. 61 in., W. 33½ in., D. 42 in.

Signed on underside of cornice at back: "Edward / Zucca / 1989"
Gift of Anne and Ronald Abramson
1989.263

Edward Zucca was one of the first studio furnituremakers to successfully reach beyond the
inherent beauty of wood to focus upon hu-
mor, satire, and irony. His ability to do so
without sacrificing design or structural integrity makes him a pivotal figure in the transformation from woodworking to furnituremaking that characterizes the development of the
second generation of American studio
furnituremakers.[1]

 A graduate of the Philadelphia College of
Art, Zucca studied woodworking with Dan
Jackson, metalworking with Olaf Skoogfors,
and ceramics with Bill Daley. Jackson emphasized that students learn traditional and appropriate construction techniques, but use
them to create a contemporary aesthetic.[2] After graduation, Zucca worked initially in the
heavily carved and shaped manner of Jackson. After a trip to Mexico in 1971, however,
Zucca took a greater interest in design, drawing his vocabulary from a wide range of objects that include pre-Columbian architecture,
Egyptian material culture, Shaker furniture,
Art Deco design, appliance and car design,
and space fantasy toys of the 1940s and
1950s. Regardless of inspiration, he creates
expressive furniture that balances design and
structural integrity.

 XVIIIth Dynasty Television manifests
Zucca's satirical fascination with Egyptian
material. Responding to the hype that sur-
rounded the blockbuster exhibition of King
Tut's treasures, Zucca drew inspiration from
an actual object from that tomb to create a
modern media center. He used the Tut sled as
a console for a symbolic, nonfunctional tele-

vision, replete with gold-leafed sun disc
screen and rush-covered speaker screen. The
faux-patinated half-moon antenna and hiero-
glyphic representation of the electrical cord
and control knobs further demonstrate how
Zucca borrowed materials and motifs from
the period, but rearranged them or adapted
them to make social commentary in a humor-
ous, non-threatening manner. His television is
rich in its various layers – materials, techniques, creative idea, and edge – and attests
to the strength of furnituremaking in the visual arts of the late 1980s.
E.S.C.

1. For more information on Zucca and his role in
the development of studio furniture, see Edward S.
Cooke, Jr., *New American Furniture* (Boston: Museum of Fine Arts, Boston, 1989), pp. 19-31 and
128-131.

2. Nancy Corwin, "Vital Connections: The Furniture of Daniel Jackson," *American Craft* 50, no. 3
(June/July 1990), pp. 50-55 and 74-75.

Rosanne Somerson
(b. 1954)

28.
Bench (exh. no. 112)
Westport, Massachusetts, 1986
Pearwood, soft curly maple, leather
H. 22¾ in., W. 57½ in., D. 22¼ in.

Signed on underside of front rail: "Assisted by D.E.K. 8 RS (intertwined with the s surmounting the R) 6 FOR MFA Thanks to R.A. + A.A."
Gift of Anne and Ronald Abramson 1987.40

Although such woodworkers as Sam Maloof and the late George Nakashima were primarily self-taught, their work led to the development of several academic programs in furniture design and construction. The cumulative technical expertise developed over the last forty years and the increasing analytical and critical dialogue initiated by the college programs led to the flourishing of studio furniture in the 1980s. Rosanne Somerson is one of the most productive and articulate leaders of the contemporary studio furniture movement. A graduate of the Rhode Island School of Design, she has influenced the woodworking field through her furniture, lectures and workshops, editorial work for *Fine Woodworking*, and teaching at RISD. She builds graceful forms with traditional materials, layers of detail, and delightful decoration to entice the user or viewer to react, think, or imagine.[1]

Somerson's work all manifests a concern with structural strength and a sophisticated sense of graphic design. She strives to build furniture that will continue to please and engage. Within the past four years she has produced a series of benches, couches, and daybeds that possess a subtle formality with small-scale shaped details. Using different sorts of woods, varying decorative finishes such as paint or carving, and upholstering the seats with different colored woven material or leather, she has explored the couch form fully. This particular bench, distinguished by its exquisite applied decoration and harmonious relationship between wood frame and leather cover, is her most successful version. Previ-

ously she had sketched many pieces with marquetry decoration, but had never actually used the pictorial technique. For this couch she applied three-dimensional relief carving. She set small, cut-out and shaped "jewels" of quiet solid wood within a rail of rich solid wood that serves as a frame. She then covered the seat with deeply colored blue leather that complements the pearwood frame.
E.S.C.

1. Edward S. Cooke, Jr., *New American Furniture* (Boston: Museum of Fine Arts, Boston, 1989), esp. pp. 116-119.

Mark Lindquist
(b. 1949)

29.
Ascending Bowl #12 (exh. no. 115)
Quincy, Florida, 1988
American black walnut
H. 14¼ in., DIAM. (rim) 17¾ in.

Signed on base: "Mark Lindquist / 1988 /
Ascending Bowl / #12 / Walnut"
Gift of Mr. and Mrs. Sidney Stoneman
1989.205

The revival of woodturning as a craft began
in the 1950s with James Prestini's perfect,
seamless bowls and plates that emphasized
the geometric perfection of form. Since the
late 1970s, the craft has seen an increasingly
diverse range of artists who have sought to
use the lathe in more creative ways.

Foremost among these is Mark Lindquist,
the son of accomplished turner Melvin Lindquist, who has gone beyond the vessel form to
blur the distinction between turning and
sculpture. Lindquist's work is informed by an
Asian sensibility that tempers his attitude toward technical perfection and fosters his respect for the physical spirit of each unique cut
of wood.[1] Lindquist is unique among his contemporaries in his fundamentally sculptural
approach to the wooden vessel, and uses an
elaborate sequence of tools, particularly the
lathe and chainsaw along with others of his
own design, to achieve his ends.

Ascending Bowl #12's compelling presence
can be partially attributed to its scale, as developed with Lindquist's ruggedly sculptural
approach. After initially turning the wood,
Lindquist raked the exterior with a turning
skew on end, thereby raising the wood grain.
He then wire-brushed the surface to soften its
appearance. The result is simultaneously
rough and velvety smooth. In a radical departure from even the most innovative techniques, Lindquist used a specially rigged
chainsaw to cut the center of the bowl while
it was wet, leaving angled chasms as he
worked.[2] Taken as a whole, the bowl's large
and rough-hewn appearance gives the impres-
sion that it was made by giants.
J.J.F.

1. Lindquist explains his techniques and provides
thoughtful commentary on woodturning in his insightful *Sculpting Wood: Contemporary Tools and
Techniques* (Worcester, Mass.: Davis Publications,
1986).

2. Telephone conversation between the artist and
the author, 6 June 1989.

Horatio Greenough
(1805-1852)

30.
Arno (exh. no. 59)
Florence, Italy, 1839
Marble
H. 25½ in., D. 22½ in., L. 51½ in.
Arthur Tracy Cabot Fund 1972.601

Boston-born and Harvard-educated, Horatio Greenough settled in Florence in 1825 and studied with Lorenzo Bartolini at the Academia de Belle Arti. The United States Congress commissioned the twenty-seven-year-old Greenough to make a colossal marble of George Washington, the pose of which was inspired by a nineteenth-century reconstruction of Phidias's *Olympian Zeus*. The first large-scale marble made by an American in the Greek revival manner, it was shipped to America in 1841, but received mixed reviews. Many were perplexed and even offended by the partial nudity of the father of the country.[1]

The Museum of Fine Arts is fortunate to own eleven examples of Greenough's sculpture, most of them small in scale and nearly all by gift from Mrs. Greenough late in the nineteenth century.[2] *Arno*, the most recent ac-

quisition, is one of the sculptor's most compelling works, for it enabled him to express his artistic theories free from the conventions of idealizing human form according to the canons of classical antiquity. Embodied in this study is the principle of opposition – that of stillness versus motion or repose versus action. Although the dog is at rest, he is alert, prepared for swift motion. For Greenough, beauty had no arbitrary law of proportion or unbending model of form. In contrast to the eighteenth-century notions of beauty articulated by Edmund Burke, who found beauty in things small, smooth, soft, round and feminine, Greenough proposed that beauty could be defined as the promise of function. In articulating the principles of beauty, form, and function he stated, "The horse's shanks are thin, and we admire them; the greyhound's chest is deep, and we cry, beautiful!"[3] Greenough was an early functionalist as well as an eloquent champion of the importance of art in America. At his death in 1852 fellow artists accorded him the title of "Pioneer of American Sculpture."

The famous statesman and orator, Edward Everett, purchased *Arno* after it had passed through three owners' hands subsequent to its arrival in Boston in 1840. For many years it

graced a corner of his drawing-room in Cambridge and later his library in Boston. It was subsequently purchased by Quincy sculptor John Horrigan (1864-1939), who left it to his son, Gerald, also a sculptor. While working as a guard at the Museum late in his life, Gerald noticed a revived interest in American neoclassical sculpture and sold the marble to the Museum in 1973.

J.L.F.

1. It was moved outside the Capitol and in recent years was installed within the Museum of American History in Washington, D.C. On this commission, see Wayne Craven, "Horatio Greenough's Statue of Washington and Phidias's *Olympian Zeus*," *Art Quarterly*, 26 (Winter, 1963), pp. 429-440.

2. Jan Seidler Ramirez, "Horatio Greenough" in *American Figurative Sculpture in the Museum of Fine Arts, Boston*, (Boston: Museum of Fine Arts, Boston, 1986), pp. 4-26, see fig. 12.

3. Harold A. Small ed., *Form and Function: Remarks on Art, by Horatio Greenough* (Berkeley: University of California Press, 1947) p. 58. For a more extensive view of Greenough's theories see "Relative and Independent Beauty," "Burke on the Beautiful," "Criticism in Search of Beauty," and "Structure and Organization" in Henry T. Tuckerman, *A Memorial of Horatio Greenough* (New York: G.P. Putnam & Co., 1853), pp. 131-183.

Thomas Crawford
(1813-1857)

31.
Orpheus and Cerberus (exh. no. 78)
Rome, Italy, 1839 (modeled) 1843 (carved)
Marble
H. 67½ in., W. 36 in., D. 54 in.

Inscribed on base, left: T.G.CRAWFORD,
FECIT./ROMAE/MDCCCXLIII
Gift of Mr. and Mrs. Cornelius Vermeule III
1975.800

In the 1840s Boston residents loved to claim
that their town was the "Athens of America,"
and Thomas Crawford's sculpture of *Orpheus
and Cerberus* is the single most eloquent reminder of neoclassicism in Boston. Before de-
parting for Rome in 1839 he had already
gained a practical knowledge of modeling in
clay and carving in stone in his native New
York. After a year of study in Rome with
world-celebrated Danish sculptor Bertel
Thorvaldsen (1770-1844), Crawford boldly
struck out on his own, attempting to distill
the Greek spirit into modern classical forms
that avoided the extravagant gestures and
elaborate "S" curves characteristic of earlier
baroque and rococo art.[1]

Orpheus, Crawford's first major sculpture,
was clearly the turning point in his career.
Early in 1839 he began designs for the theme,
which came from the tenth book of Ovid's
Metamorphoses. Orpheus left the realms of
light and upper air to venture into the underworld and seek his lost love, Eurydice. Crawford portrays the moment when Orpheus,
having lulled to sleep the three-headed dog
Cerberus, by playing his lyre, rushes trium-
phantly through the gates of hell in search of
his Eurydice. For inspiration of form he
turned to what was then believed to be the
most important masterpiece of antique sculpture, the *Apollo Belvedere* in the Vatican.

George Washington Greene, the American
consul in Rome was an influential friend and
valuable supporter, and felt Crawford was the
modern Phidias. Senator Charles Sumner of
Massachusetts, who met Crawford in Rome
while the sculpture was in process, also provided essential help. Upon his return to Boston, Sumner helped to raise subscriptions to
make a marble version of the model. The
carving was accomplished between 1841 and
1843, and the marble was shipped to the Boston Athenaeum.[2] *Orpheus and Cerberus* went
on public view in a special exhibition space
on 6 May 1844, and received high critical acclaim. As a result of this successful exhibition,
Crawford received a number of commissions,
the most prominent being the posthumously
completed "Armed Liberty" atop the U.S.
Capitol and *Hebe and Ganymede* (76.702),
given to the Museum in 1876.

Orpheus and Cerberus remained at the
Athenaeum until 1872 when it went on loan
to the newly founded Museum of Fine Arts
where it stayed for more than one hundred
years.[3] The Athenaeum's unexpected with-
drawal of the *Orpheus and Cerberus* loan in
1975 prompted the noted scholars of classical
art, Drs. Cornelius and Emily Vermeule, to
make a generous gift to the Museum of Crawford's great debut piece. This gift reflects the
Vermeules' understanding of the revival of
classicism in American art and the unique
role played by *Orpheus and Cerberus* in
bringing the Greek revival to Boston.
J.L.F.

1. Lauretta Dimmick, "Thomas Crawford's Orpheus: The American Apollo Belvedere", *The
American Art Journal*, vol. XIX no. 4, 1987, pp.

47-84; and Jan Seidler Ramirez, "Thomas Crawford" in *American Figurative Sculpture in the Museum of Fine Arts, Boston*, (Boston: Museum of
Fine Arts, Boston, 1986), pp. 52-66.

2. When the sculpture was uncrated in 1843 it was
found broken across the knees, ankles and dog.
Henry Dexter (1806-1876), a local sculptor, performed a remarkable restoration of the work by
drilling a three inch hole through the entire length
of Cerberus, fitting a copper shaft through that tun-
nel, and bolting the sculpture completely together
with a large nut on the shaft at the underside of the
marble. After pinning all parts of the work together,
he masked with tinted plaster all the repairs so that
they can not be easily discerned.

3. Early photographs of the entrance hall to the
Museum on Copley Square show *Orpheus and Cerberus* facing opposite *Hebe and Ganymede* and
Crawford's portrait of Charles Sumner flanking the
central staircase.

William Wetmore Story
(1819-1895)

32.
Sappho (exh. no. 79)
Rome, 1863
Marble
H. 54⅞ in., W. 32⅛ in., D. 34 in.
Signed on back: WWS/ROMA 1863
Otis Norcross Fund 1977.772

When William Wetmore Story completed his model for this carving, he wrote to his friend and critic, Charles Eliot Norton, "I fancy just at this moment of time that you would think it my best work – I have put all the love into it I could." He described it further as being "very tender, very sweet, very sentimental."[1] Story was a world-famous literary figure and sculptor when he made it. He had just received lavish praise for the two seated marble females he displayed at the 1862 London Exposition: *Cleopatra* and the *Lybian Sibyl*. For Story the monumental brooding female figure became a highly successful sculptural archetype that held vast appeal to Victorians. He subsequently modelled and had carved monumental figures of Sappho, Delilah, Judith, Salome, Medea, Semiramis, and Jerusalem in her Desolation – all historic women or symbolic types whose troubled lives and personal drama were understood by Victorians educated in the classics.[2]

According to Ovid, Sappho, poetess of the Island of Lesbos, was so depressed by the unrequited love of Greek ferryboatman Phaon that she hurled herself off the cliffs of Leucadia into the sea. With this marble, Story depicts Sappho in a listless reverie before flinging her necklace and then herself into the sea. Her harp is laid aside, a rose wilts. The symbolism is clear: without love, creativity is lost. The sculpture is a metaphor for the Muses.[3]

An accomplished author, critic and classicist, Story had already been commissioned to create a memorial to his late father, Chief Justice Joseph Story, before he travelled to Rome in 1845 to study sculpture. He spent the rest of his life in Rome, where Story's apartment in the Palazzo Barberini was the center for visits from such friends as Nathaniel Hawthorne, Margaret Fuller, Robert and Elizabeth Browning and William Makepeace Thackeray.

While Henry James believed that the diversity of Story's talents crippled his voice as a sculptor, and Lorado Taft, a later sculptor, also dismissed Story's sculptural accomplishments, new scholarship suggests that Story's work was much more significant than previously believed. In contrast to the neoclassicism of Horatio Greenough, Thomas Crawford and Hiram Powers, Story's more robust eclecticism incorporated complex literary, symbolic, and mystical themes.

J.L.F.

1. William Wetmore Story to Charles Eliot Norton, May 3, 1862, Charles Eliot Norton Papers, Houghton Library, Harvard University, Cambridge, Massachusetts. See also Jan Seidler Ramirez, "William Wetmore Story," in *American Figurative Sculpture in the Museum of Fine Arts, Boston* (Boston: Museum of Fine Arts, Boston, 1986), pp. 107-130.

2. Jan Seidler Ramirez, "The 'Lovelorn Lady': A New Look at William Wetmore Story's *Sappho*," The American Art Journal (Summer 1983), pp. 81-90.

3. Jan. M. Seidler, "A Critical Reappraisal of the Career of William Wetmore Story (1819-1895), American Sculptor and Man of Letters" (PhD diss., Boston University, 1985).

ing brow with ample space between the eyes, and deep-set eyes open with wonder. The space between the lower end of the nose and the upper edge of the lip is very small, and a prominent nose keeps the portrait from being merely pretty. The lips are open as if with surprise, and the chin is generous without being rugged.

J.L.F.

1. This *Head of Victory* is one of two owned by the Museum. The second seems likely to have been cast after the sculptor's death. Together they offer the connoisseur intriguing comparisons, as the one on view is by far more artfully cast and colored. See Kathryn Greenthal, *Augustus Saint-Gaudens, Master Sculptor* (New York: The Metropolitan Museum of Arts, 1985); and Kathryn Greenthal, "Augustus Saint-Gaudens" in *American Figurative Sculpture in the Museum of Fine Arts, Boston*, (Boston: Museum of Fine Arts, Boston, 1986), pp. 214-249.

Augustus Saint-Gaudens
(1848-1907)

33.
Head of Victory (exh. no. 80)
Paris or New York, about 1907
Bronze, marble
H. 8 in., w. 7 in., D. 6¼ in.

Signed on proper left side of neck: A. SAINT GAVDENS. M•C•MV.
Helen and Alice Colburn Fund 1977.600 Augustus Saint-Gaudens transformed American sculpture by moving away from the marble traditions of neoclassicism toward boldly modeled bronzes of the Beaux-Arts style. After Saint-Gaudens, progressive American artists of the late nineteenth century trained in France rather than Italy and centered their studios and much of their work in the city of New York rather than Boston or New England. As a result, the Museum's collection is much stronger in neoclassical marbles than in American Renaissance bronzes, with the exception of work by Saint-Gaudens.

The Museum's distinguished collection of works by Saint-Gaudens includes eleven works acquired before the Department began collecting, and six added since 1971. Of these, *Head of Victory* is the most compelling sculpture in the round . It represents a study for the idealized head of the bronze figure that leads the equestrian Sherman Monument in the city of New York, the last of Saint-Gaudens's heroic public monuments.[1]

Saint-Gaudens used idealized female figures for symbolic purposes. In this head and its many variants on coins, reliefs and other models, Saint-Gaudens struggled to attain the right balance between personal and universal attributes. While the facial features of Saint Gaudens's ideal female heads tend to be markedly similar, this one has a broad droop-

Herbert Adams
(1858-1945)

34.
The Debutante (exh. no. 96)
New York, New York, 1914
Bronze, original wooden base
H. 14½ in., w. 4½ in., D. 4½ in.

Signed: HA MCMXIV
Marked: "ROMAN BRONZE WORKS NY"
Gift of Jean S. and Frederic A. Sharf
1988.486

At the turn of the century, Herbert Adams was a leading American sculptor. Accomplished in portraits, monuments, and architectural commissions, he was a master of aesthetic decorative effects with both personal likeness and universal idealization. He is best known for his portraits of beautiful women, works with softly modulated surfaces and rich coloration or "soul atmosphere" as one critic described Adams's tender sympathy for humanity.[1]

Adams studied in Paris for five years at the Ecole des Beaux-Arts. Under Michel Louis Victor Mercier, Adams developed his natural sense of delicately handled surface modeling into a personal style of harmonic rendering of light and shade. Study at the Louvre also brought him under the spell of fifteenth-century Italian sculpture by Benedetto da Maiano (1442-1497) and the della Robbias, both Andrea (1435-1525) and Luca (about 1400-1482) of Florence.[2]

In Boston, the most prominent work by Adams is a bronze portrait monument to William Ellery Channing (1902) that stands at the corner of Arlington and Boylston Streets at the edge of the Public Gardens. As with most of Adams's sculpture, this composition emphasizes decorative features and disposition of parts within the American Renaissance tradition. Adams was elected President of the National Sculpture Society, president of the National Academy of Design, and member of the National Commission of Fine Arts in Washington.[3] After his death the National Sculpture Society established the Herbert Adams memorial medal, to be awarded for outstanding service to American sculpture.

The Debutante, a small polychrome bronze of 1914, embodies the Renaissance style popular at that time. The figure blends the affected trappings of Parisian fashion with form inspired by Florentine art. Adams returned to the debutante theme several times with other later models in 1920, 1924, 1935 and 1943 but never with the success of this first version. The Museum's bronze merges lyrical decorative composition with subtle tonal variety: the figure's face, hands, and hair are a warm bronze tone, the base is deep brown, while the gown and shoes are a muted green.

J.L.F.

1. Sadakichi Hartmann, *A History of American Art, New Revised Edition* (New York: Tudor Publishing Company, 1934) p. 73.
2. Charles H. Caffin, *American Masters of Sculpture* (Garden City, N.Y.: Doubleday, Page & Company, 1913), pp. 99-115.
3. Ernest Peixotto, "The Sculpture of Herbert Adams," *The American Magazine of Art*, XII (May 1921), p. 159.

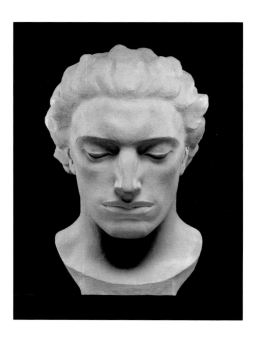

Katharine Lane Weems
(1899-1989)

35.
Revolt (exh. no. 97)
Boston, Massachusetts, 1980 (modeled in 1926)
Bronze
H. 30½ in., L. 19¼ in., D. 6 in.

Foundry mark (on top of base, front): TX (of Tallux)
Signed (on top of base, front): 19 c 80 K.
LANE WEEMS
Gift of Katharine Lane Weems 1981.664

Known mainly for such animal sculpture as the monumental *Dolphins of the Sea* (1979) at the New England Aquarium, Boston, and the life-size *Rhinocerous* (1937) made for the Harvard Biological Laboratories, Cambridge, Katharine Lane Weems also modeled human figures, portraits, medals, decorative fountains, and heroic monuments. The breadth of her work is documented by numerous sculptures willed to the Museum at her death.[1] Her art, and that of many of her contemporaries and associates of the National Sculpture Society, has been grossly underrated by serious students of art history.[2]

In 1927 the Museum acquired two of Weems's works, a pigmy *African Elephant*, which won a bronze medal at the Philadelphia Sesqui-Centennial Exhibition of 1926 and her bronze whippet, *Narcisse Noir*, which in the year following won the coveted George B. Widener Medal at the Pennsylvania Academy of the Fine Arts, Philadelphia.

Modeled in 1926, his piece was originally entitled *Striding Amazon* to symbolize femi-

nine athletic prowess at a time when social convention prevented women from achieving athletic success. After altering the plaster model in 1980, Weems renamed it *Revolt*, as an expression, perhaps, of the frustration of working in a predominantly male profession.[3] In 1981, the plaster figure was awarded the Kalos Kaganthos Foundation's prize at the National Sculpture Society's annual exhibition.

J.L.F.

1. The bequest is principally composed of over a hundred plaster studio models of animals, human portraits, reliefs and some plaster molds. Included also are medallic arts, models and sketches, art reference books and small bronzes by fellow sculptors of the National Sculpture Society. This gift provides scholars with an opportunity for in-depth study of the evolving style and working method of the sculptor.

2. Weems's career is best documented by Louise Todd Ambler, *Katharine Lane Weems, Sculpture and Drawings*. (Boston, The Boston Athenaeum, 1987). See also Jan Seidler Ramirez, "Katharine Lane Weems," in *American Figurative Sculpture in the Museum of Fine Arts, Boston* (Boston: Museum of Fine Arts, Boston, 1986), pp. 455-464.

3. Katharine Lane Weems, as told to Edward Weeks. *Odds Were Against Me: A Memoir*, New York, Vantage Press, 1985.

Walker Hancock
(b. 1901)

36.
Head of an Angel (exh. no. 98)
Lanesville, Massachusetts, 1950
Plaster
H. 32½ in., W. 21 in., D. 27 in.

Signed on proper left, bottom: Walker Hancock 1950
Gift of Walker Hancock 1980.426

Walker Hancock, whose career spans more than seventy years, is the senior American sculptor working within the figurative tradition that began with Horatio Greenough's study in Italy in the 1830s. Like Greenough, Hancock is an artist-scholar thoroughly conversant with the major movements of Western art since ancient times. But unlike Greenough, Hancock addresses contemporary issues within the context of a classical sculptural vocabulary.[1]

Hancock's most admired public war memorial is the forty-foot-high bronze figural composition dedicated in 1952 at the Thirtieth Street Railroad Station, Philadelphia. It is known as the Pennsylvania Railroad War Memorial and honors more than thirteen hundred employees of the railroad who perished in World War II. The Pennsylvania Railroad Commission began in 1948 with a series of

small sketches made by Hancock, from which the board of directors made selections. The composition agreed upon evolved into a monumental angel with soaring vertical wings lifting a dead soldier from the flames of battle. Two grand columns frame this composition.

The plaster head shown here is the original model from which the bronze at the station was cast. An ideal type representing no particular race or person, the head has the vigor found in archaic Greek sculpture. Unlike Saint-Gaudens's ideal head of Fame, Hancock's angel is neither male nor female, and its surfaces are not treated with the plasticity popular with Saint-Gaudens and his followers. The angel's face is meditative, even brooding in its expression.

The success of Hancock's public sculpture is due in part to his attentiveness to the settings for which his works are commissioned. While developing the model for the whole monument, he had full-scale photographs placed in the station. Observing the effect, Hancock made substantial changes to the full-scale monument in clay before casting was complete.

J.L.F.

1. Kathryn Greenthal and Paula M. Kozol, "Walker Hancock," in *American Figurative Sculpture in the Museum of Fine Arts, Boston*, (Boston: Museum of Fine Arts, Boston, 1986), pp. 465-468.

CERAMICS

American China Manufactory
(1770-72)

37. (color plate)
Fruit Basket (exh. no. 41)
Philadelphia, Pennsylvania, 1771-1772
Soft-paste porcelain, underglaze blue
decoration
H. 2¹¹/₁₆ in., D. 6⅞ in.

Marked: "Z"
Frederick Brown Fund 1977.621

In 1770 in Southwark, Philadelphia, Gousse Bonnin and George Anthony Morris built the first factory in North America for the large-scale production of "American China." The climate seemed ideal for such a factory in the Colonies, as the Nonimportation Agreements of the late 1760s were intended to boycott British goods and stimulate domestic manufacture. Bonnin and Morris imported skilled workers from England to produce ware comparable in style and quality to the soft-paste or bone china produced in such English factories as Bow. However, they vastly underestimated the capital investments for land, equipment, materials and a skilled workforce and did not anticipate that local merchants would not uniformly follow the Nonimportation Agreements. As increasing numbers of merchants resumed trade with England, the market became flooded with English and Chinese wares of better quality at prices far lower than those of the new factory. Within two years of opening, the American China Manufactory closed, leaving the craftsmen the principle losers of this trade war.[1]

The few surviving products of the American China Manufactory demonstrate a consistency of workmanship and fashionable design. Of the several forms produced – sweetmeat dishes, sauceboats, potpourri baskets, inkwells, cups, creampots, tureens, saucers, pickle trays and bowls – the most artistically successful is the open fretwork fruit basket. This example descended from Daniel Whitehead (1751-1792) to Thomas Willett Whitehead (1790-1871), subsequently to Annie Whitehead who married Horace G. Richards, whose son and daughter Horace Gardner Richards and Marie Richards inherited it. In 1965, when performing some analytical experiments to determine the composition of the body of an almost identical basket in the Winterthur Collection, I discovered this basket in the Richardses' family china cupboard in West Philadelphia. A second basket in the Richards family, virtually a mate to this one, is now owned by the Detroit Institute of Arts. Both baskets bear an underglaze letter "Z" on their base.[2] Others are marked "P," presumably for Philadelphia.

J.L.F.

1. For the complete story of the American China Factory, see Graham Hood, *Bonnin and Morris of Philadelphia, The First American Porcelain Factory, 1770-1772* (Williamsburg, Va.: The Institute of Early American History and Culture, 1972); and Graham Hood, "The American China," in Francis J. Puig, and Michael Comforti, eds., *The American Craftsman and the European Tradition, 1620-1820* (Minneapolis, Minn.: The Minneapolis Institute of Arts, 1989), pp. 240-255.
2. Perhaps the "Z" marks are a decorator's initial rather than a misinterpreted "S" for the Southwark site.

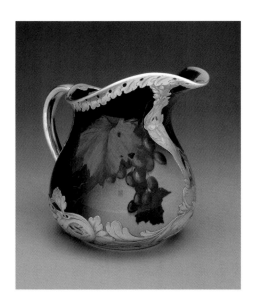

Rookwood Pottery Company
(1880-1960)

Gorham Manufacturing Company
(1831-)

38.
Pitcher (exh. no. 72)
Decorated by Constance Amelia Baker (active 1892-1904)
Cincinnati, Ohio, 1894
White earthenware, decorated with brown, yellow, green, and blue slip and covered with transparent glossy glaze; silver deposit decoration
H. 6⅝ in., W. 8¼ in., D. 6 in.

Marked: "(seven flames) / R (reversed) P" / 52 D / W. Signed on base: "CAB." Marked on silver: "R1056 GORHAM MFG CO."
Edwin E. Jack Fund 1989.200

In Cincinnati, Ohio, the decorative arts blossomed during the last quarter of the nineteenth century. Maria Longworth Nichols was one of a small core of dedicated women artists there whose work affected the course of the Arts and Crafts movement on a national scale.[1]

Deeply impressed by the Japanese and Chinese ceramics that she saw at the Pennsylvania Centennial Exposition of 1876, Nichols returned home determined to create her own vessels. She established Rookwood Pottery Company in order to provide training for young artists and a creative atmosphere in which accomplished craftsmen could flourish. She encouraged experimentation in designs and glazes, and received numerous awards for her efforts, including a gold medal at the 1889 Universal Exposition in Paris.[2]

This pitcher is executed in Rookwood's Standard style, typically a blend of warm

brown, yellow, red, and green slip colors applied with a mouth aspirator or air brush and covered with a transparent glaze. The bunch of grapes with leaves complements the shape of the pitcher and is accentuated by an exuberant, floral silver-deposit decoration by Gorham Manufacturing Company. The silver-deposit process, which employed graphite in a plating technique on the normally nonconductive ceramic, was used by Rookwood primarily on their Standard style pottery. The technique was popular for about ten years following the Chicago Columbian Exposition of 1893.[3]
J.J.F.

1. The best survey on women artists in Cincinnati at the turn of the century is *The Ladies, God Bless 'Em: The Women's Art Movement in Cincinnati in the Nineteenth Century* (Cincinnati: Cincinnati Art Museum, 1976).

2. Paul Evans, "Rookwood Pottery," in *Art Pottery of the United States* (New York: Feingold & Lewis Publishing Corp., 1987), pp. 255-260 (387). For an examination of the Japanese influence on Rookwood, see Kenneth Trapp, "Rookwood and the Japanese Mania in Cincinnati," *Cincinnati Historical Society Bulletin* 39 (Spring 1981), pp. 51-75.

3. For a discussion of silver deposit techniques, see Charles H. Carpenter, Jr., *Gorham Silver 1831-1981* (New York: Dodd, Mead & Company, 1982), pp. 215-217.

Newcomb Pottery
(1895-1940)

39.
Vase (exh. no. 87)
Thrown by Joseph Fortune Meyer (1848-1931)
Decorated by Marie (d. 1954) and Emilie de Hoa LeBlanc (d. 1941)
New Orleans, Louisiana, 1902
Buff colored earthenware with blue-green glossy glaze
H. 11⅜ in., DIAM. (rim) 3⅝ in.

Marks: incised on bottom: conjoined cipher of JM, cipher of ELEB, Q; painted in blue underglaze: N with C cipher, conjoined cipher of M-LeB, and W44
Laurie Crichton Memorial Fund 1980.226

Ellsworth Woodward established Newcomb Pottery in 1895 at Newcomb College, the women's college at Tulane University in New Orleans, where he employed art students as staff decorators upon graduation. Like other potteries of the period, Newcomb employed a division of labor where male potters worked the clay, threw the pots, fired the kiln, and mixed the glazes, while women decorators designed and painted the surfaces of the vessels. Mary Given Sheerer (1865-1954), who received her

training at the Cincinnati Art Academy and had taught pottery and china decoration at the College, supervised the decorating staff. Inspired by the local natural environment, the decorative designs were simple and bold. Sheerer emphasized that "the whole thing was to be a southern product, made of southern clays, by southern artists, decorated with southern subjects!"[1] Cool colored glazes of blues and greens, as in this work, were frequently used by Newcomb. In adherence to the philosophies of the Arts and Crafts movement, each piece was uniquely designed and executed. This vessel typifies Newcomb ware before 1910. With the arrival of Paul E. Cox, Newcomb's first professionally trained ceramic engineer, the characteristic high-gloss glaze would be displaced by the popular matte glaze used by other potteries.

By 1898 Newcomb Pottery began participating in annual national and international expositions. In the following year this museum became one of the first to acquire Newcomb Pottery. Between 1900 and 1915 Newcomb Pottery received awards at eight international expositions. The Louisiana Purchase Exposition at Saint Louis in 1904 featured twenty-three Newcomb pieces; the potter of this elegant vase won a silver medal, and Marie de Hoa LeBlanc won a bronze medal for her painting and glazing.

Marie LeBlanc's designs were typically vertical in thrust and highly stylized. She and her older sister Emilie worked together in the Pottery Design department from about 1901 to 1905.[2]
M.P.

1. Mary G. Sheerer, "Newcomb Pottery," *Keramic Studio*, vol. 1 (November 1899), pp. 151-152.

2. For general information on Newcomb Pottery consult Paul Evans, *Art Pottery of the United States*, (New York: Feingold & Lewis Publishing Corp., 1987), pp. 182-187. Data on Newcomb Pottery, their potters and craftsmen was gleaned from Jessie Poesch, *Newcomb Pottery: An Enterprise for Southern Women, 1895-1940*, (Exton, Pennsylvania: Schiffer Publishing Limited, 1984).

Grueby-Faience Company (1894-1909) or Grueby Faience and Tile Company (1909-1920)

40.
Tile (exh. no. 88)
Designed by Addison B. Le Boutillier (1872-1951)
Boston, Massachusetts, 1906-20
Light buff earthenware with matte glaze
H. 8⅟₁₆ in., w. 8⅟₁₆ in., D. 1 in.

Marked on back: "GRUEBY/BOSTON"
Gift of C. Malcolm and Joan P. Watkins in Memory of Lura Woodside Watkins
1987.662

Art pottery produced during the late nineteenth and early twentieth centuries reflected the Arts and Crafts movement's reaction against the mass-produced, uniform, and sterile works manufactured since the Industrial Revolution. By 1870 craftsmen rebelled against industrial ceramics by establishing commercial art potteries, where artists and technicians worked together to produce unique works. Lura Woodside Watkins (1887-1982) collected works by a number of New England art potteries; this fine Grueby tile is one of forty-six works in her collection, which was generously given to the Museum by her son C. Malcolm and his wife Joan P. Watkins.

Art potteries like those established by William Henry Grueby (1867-1925) favored simplicity of form and color over the elaborate shapes and extensive decoration of the Victorian era. Grueby worked for and later established companies best known for their hand-thrown vases and tiles made of clays from New Jersey and Martha's Vineyard. The works were decorated by women graduates of the School of The Museum of Fine Arts, Boston, the Massachusetts Normal School (now Massachusetts College of Art), and the Cowles Art School. Grueby popularized the use of matte glazes and his cucumber green

glaze, in particular, was widely admired and imitated.

The early Grueby architectural tiles were inspired by Moorish style, Luca della Robbia and Donatello ceramics, and Chinese tiles. Typical tile images included tulips, lilies, ships, and pine tree landscapes such as that on this tile, designed by architect Addison B. Le Boutillier.

Le Boutillier, who became head designer when George Prentiss Kendrick left the firm in 1901, made three major contributions to Grueby ware. He introduced classic oriental-shaped vases, more delicately modeled decoration, and simplified pottery shapes. Influenced by ancient European tiles, Le Boutillier favored irregular shaped forms, soft glazed decoration, and designs that would blend and enhance, rather than dominate its environment.[1] While this delicate landscape is very similar to Le Boutillier's popular "The Pines" frieze of eight tiles decorated with a continuous landscape of pine trees, this tile is not part of that series, but an individual tile.[2] By 1920, the Grueby Faience and Tile Company, like other art potteries, was experiencing financial difficulty because the high cost of producing hand-made works made them non-competitive with industrial wares.
M.P.

1. For information on the art pottery movement and the Grueby potteries see Paul Evans, *Art Pottery of the United States*, (New York: Feingold & Lewis Publishing Corp., 1987), pp. 1-8 and 118-123; and Martin Eidelberg, "The Ceramic Art of William H. Grueby," *The Connoisseur*, vol. 184, no. 739 (September 1973), pp. 47-54. Information on Le Boutillier gleaned from Neville Thompson, "Addison B. Le Boutillier: Developer of Grueby Tiles," *Tiller*, vol. 1, no. 2 (November - December 1982), pp. 21-30 and Clark Pearce with research by Neville Thompson, *Addison B. Le Boutillier: Andover Artist and Craftsman*, exhibition catalogue (Andover: Andover Historical Society, 1987), pp. 15-25.

2. The author would like to thank Susan Montgomery for information with regard to this tile and "The Pines" series.

1. The three primary publications that summarize Marblehead pottery are Martin Eidelberg "Art Pottery" in *The Arts and Crafts Movement in America 1876-1916* (Princeton, N.J.: Princeton University Press, 1972), p. 180; Paul Evans, *Art Pottery of the United States* (N.Y.: Feingold and Lewis Pub. Corp., 1987), pp. 157-160, and Wendy Kaplan, ed. *"The Art that is Life": The Arts and Crafts Movement in America 1875-1920* (Boston: Little, Brown and Company, 1987), cat. 115-116.

2. Peg Weiss, ed. *Adelaide Alsop Robineau, Glory in Porcelain* (Syracuse: Syracuse University Press in association with Everson Museum of Art, 1981), pp. 62, 84, fig. 106.

3. Related examples are found in Ulysses G. Dietz, *The Newark Museum Collection of American Art Pottery* (Newark, N.J.: The Newark Museum, 1984), fig. 144, and Martin Eidelberg, ed. *From our Native Clay, Art Pottery from The Collections of the American Ceramic Arts Society* (N.Y.: American Ceramic Arts Society, 1987), fig. 64.

Marblehead Pottery
(1904-1936)

41.

Bowl (exh. no. 89)
Marblehead, Massachusetts, about 1910-15
Earthenware with incised and glazed decoration
H. 3⅞ in., DIAM. 10½ in.

Stamped twice on bottom, "M (square-rigged ship) P" within circle
Gift of John P. Axelrod 1990.48

Marblehead Pottery was founded in 1904 as part of the Handcrafts Shops, a sanitorium that employed crafts as a therapeutic aid for patients suffering from nervous exhaustion. The pottery was separated from the medical facility in 1905 to better control the standards of production, and in 1908 Arthur E. Baggs (1886-1947) joined the pottery. As a former student of Charles F. Binns (1857-1934) at the New York School of Clayworking and Ceramics at Alfred, New York, Baggs received the best available practical and artistic education in the medium. He and his small staff at Marblehead Pottery became known for their high-quality wheel-thrown earthenware, matte glazes, and restrained decorative designs.[1]

Pottery designs at Marblehead were done in the conventional poster style of the time, popularized for decorators by Baggs's fellow student Adelaide Alsop Robineau (1865-1929) in her periodical *Keramic Studio*.[2] Animals and birds appeared in Marblehead pottery along with geometric and floral decorations, some of it related to the New England coast. The panther, probably Marblehead's most exotic subject, is executed in four glazes.[3] It is notable for its complex design and rich color, both remarkable from a pottery better known for its cool palette and austere simplicity of design.
J.J.F.

Cowan Pottery Studio
(1912-1931)

42. (color plate)

Punch bowl from the "Jazz Bowl" series
(exh. no. 93)
Thrown by Reginald Guy Cowan
Designed and decorated by Viktor Schreckengost (b. 1906)
Rocky River, Ohio, 1931
Glazed porcelain with sgraffito decoration
H. 9 in., DIAM. (rim) 16⅞ in.

Gift of John P. Axelrod 1990.507

American ceramics, like the other decorative arts, underwent a transformation between the world wars. The Moderne or Art Deco movement emphasized the use of modern functional designs that could be mass-produced using new materials and the use of decorative motifs drawn from such contemporary themes as the skyscraper. Designs were typically streamlined, modernistic, geometrically patterned, and highly colorful and playful. American ceramicists of this period were very much inspired by the freshness of the works by their Viennese contemporaries who disregarded traditional ceramic techniques. Viennese designer Julius Mihalik, who taught at the Cleveland School of Art, introduced his students to the Viennese ceramic sculptures of Michael Powolny and Vally Wieselthier of the Weiner Werkstätte studio. His students and other potters who worked at Cowan Pottery in Cleveland became intrigued with the idea of ceramics as sculpture rather than as vessel and thus influenced American ceramics for the next twenty years.

The most influential of this Cleveland school, which emphasized spontaneity, wit, and vitality, was Viktor Schreckengost, an internationally acclaimed potter, industrial designer, and sculptor. As a young boy, Schreckengost worked at The French China Company in Sebring, Ohio, where his father supervised the kiln firing.[1] He left pottery to study industrial design at the Cleveland School of Art from 1924 to 1929. Impressed by the ceramic sculpture of Powolny, which he saw at the traveling International Ceramic Exhibition that opened in 1929 at the Cleveland Museum of Art, Schreckengost went to Vienna to study under Powolny at the Kunstgewerbeschule.

Upon returning to the United States in 1930, Schreckengost taught at the Cleveland Institute of Art and worked as a designer for Reginald Guy Cowan at the Cowan Pottery Studio in nearby Rocky River. There he designed the series of twenty punch bowls commissioned by Eleanor Roosevelt for a party at the governor's mansion in Albany, New York. The black and Egyptian blue glazed bowls were sgraffito-decorated with motifs of New York: images of skyscrapers, champagne glasses, saxophones, moons, and stars; and words such as *jazz, dance, follies, cafe, stop*, and *go*. After the Roosevelt commission, Schreckengost refined the design and a limited edition of fifty bowls was produced by the Cowan pottery. This fine bowl is one such example from the "Jazz Bowl" series, one of the last series the influential Cowan placed into production.[2]
M.P.

1. James Stubblebine and Martin Eidelberg, "Viktor Schreckengost and the Cleveland School," *Craft Horizons*, vol. 35, no. 3 (June 1975), pp. 34.

2. Information on entry on the movement, Schreckengost, and other ceramicists of the period was gleaned from Alastair Duncan, *American Art Deco*, (New York: Harry N. Abrams, Inc., 1986).

Otto Natzler
(b. 1908)

Gertrud Amon Natzler
(1908-1971)

43.
Bowl (exh. no. 104)
Los Angeles, California, 1957
Red earthenware with gray-earth crater glaze
H. 4⅞ in., DIAM. (rim) 8⅞ in.

Signed: NATZLER; labeled: H 451
Anonymous Gift 1989.184

Unlike many American ceramicists of the
1930s, the Natzlers rejected the ornamental
ceramic sculpture of the Viennese school in
favor of a more classical style with highly decorative glazes. In fact, throughout their almost forty-year career, their work developed
outside the mainstream.

Otto Natzler and Gertrud Amon met in
1933 and briefly studied ceramics with Franz
Iskra the following year before establishing
their own ceramic studio in 1935 in their
hometown of Vienna. Reversing the division
of labor characteristic of art potteries, Gertrud threw the vessels, while Otto formulated
and applied the glazes. Primarily self-taught,
they experimented freely with materials and
techniques. After being awarded the silver
medal at the Paris International Exposition in
1937, the Natzlers emigrated to the United
States and settled in Los Angeles in 1939.
Their elegantly formed and richly glazed
works won them first prize at the Ceramic
Nationals in Syracuse later that year and
quickly established them as leading American
ceramicists.

Using a specially formulated red firing clay,
Gertrud modeled remarkably thin-walled vessels that were intimate in scale and classically
elegant in profile. Gertrud concentrated on
four basic forms: the round bowl, teardrop
bottle, double-curved bowl or bottle, and
bowl with a flaring lip, like this vessel. These
forms inspired the types of glaze that Otto
would apply.[1] The unintended pockmarks,
holes, craters, and blisters of his early work
led Otto to formulate a series of diverse glazes
inspired by nature, including his Pompeian,
Lava, Reduction, Crystalline, and Crater
glazes. He developed more than 2000 different
glazes, which he applied to the almost 25,000
vessels thrown by Gertrud. He meticulously
recorded the mixtures and firing processes of
each glaze as well as the form and dimensions
of all of their vessels with the exception of
200-300 pieces produced in early 1939.[2]
M.P.

1. D. Graeme Keith and Otto Natzler, "A Conversation with Otto Natzler," *The Ceramic Work of
Gertrud and Otto Natzler* retrospective exhibition

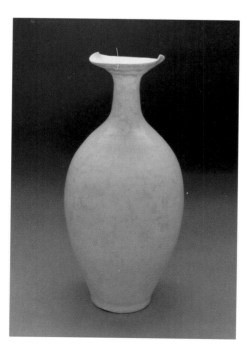

catalogue, (San Francisco: M.H. de Young Memorial Museum, July 24 - September 6, 1971).

2. Information on Natzlers's clay, glazes, forms,
model numbers as well as attitudes and philosophies on ceramics gleaned from monograph by Otto
Natzler, in *Gertrud and Otto Natzler Ceramics:
Catalog of the Collection of Mrs. Leonard M.
Sperry*, (Los Angeles: Plantin Press with Los Angeles County Museum of Art, 1968) and Otto Natzler, Preface to *The Ceramic Work of Gertrud and
Otto Natzler: A Retrospective Exhibition*, (Los Angeles County Museum of Art, Lytton Gallery, June
15-August 14, 1966).

Laura Andreson
(b. 1902)

44.
Bottle (exh. no. 105)
Los Angeles, California, 1983
Porcelain with white crystalline glaze
H. 8⅞ in.; w. 4½ in.

Scratched on base: "Laura Andreson," "83"
in circle
Gift of Mary-Louise Meyer in Memory of
Norman Meyer 1984.75

During the 1930s, when knowledge of advanced ceramic techniques and equipment in
California was restricted to a few studio potters and the art potteries, Laura Andreson
established one of the nation's first academic
ceramic programs at the University of California in Los Angeles. After graduating from
UCLA, where she was first exposed to ceramics, Andreson taught art courses there as she
pursued her masters degree in painting at Columbia University in New York.[1] By 1936 she
was teaching ceramics exclusively, and in a
short time she established herself as the leading figure in the ceramics movement of Southern California.

Andreson's early works in low-fired earthenware were either slip-cast in one- and two-
piece molds, coiled, or slab constructed by
hand; they were fired with bright glossy
glazes, popular at that time. Because high-fir-
ing stoneware clays were unavailable, Andreson experimented with matte glazes and
other firing possibilities. She learned how to
throw on a wheel in 1944 by sending students
to learn the technique from Carlton Ball, at
Mills College in Oakland, and by consulting

Gertrud Natzler in Los Angeles. Experimenting with reduction firing and the use of a potter's wheel, she developed new glaze compositions and forms.

On a world tour in 1957, Andreson visited the potteries and ceramic collections of numerous cultures, and became fascinated with porcelain. The glaze and textures of Scandinavian porcelains of the 1950s, particularly those of Stig Lindberg (b. 1916), led Andreson to abandon earthenware and stoneware to work exclusively in porcelain.[2] Andreson first creates a glaze and then the vessel form that will best complement it. The refined surface qualities of porcelain enhances the brilliance, color, and texture of her glazes. As is evident in this milky white crystalline glazed bottle, Andreson's forms are inspired by the perfection and thin shell of an egg. Unmoved by the current vogues in ceramics, Andreson has always been influenced by nature and ancient pottery.[3]
M.P.

1. For biographical information on artist see Garth Clark, *American Ceramics 1876 to the Present*, (New York: Abbeville Press, 1987), p. 251.

2. See Diana Rico, "Laura Andreson: An Interview," *American Ceramics*, vol. 3, no. 2, pp. 12-19.

3. For information on Andreson's teaching, style, and developments, see Bernard Kester introduction in *Laura Andreson: A Retrospective in Clay*, (La Jolla, California: Mingei International Museum of World Folk Art, 1982), pp. 9-12.

Brother Thomas (Thomas Bezanson) (b. 1929)

45. (color plate)
Vase (exh. no. 107)
Western Priory, Weston, Vermont, 1980
Porcelain
H. 14 in., DIAM. (max) 13 in.

Marks: £, "2/2," "802," "30/15/20/1"
Gift of Edith W. and Frederick Bloom
1981.38

After years of studying and collecting works by Brother Thomas, Edith and Frederick Bloom presented the Museum with his masterwork. Flawlessly thrown and colored with a copper red glaze, this vase is the largest and most impressive of ten porcelains by Brother Thomas owned by the Museum.[1]

Brother Thomas has been making pottery since 1953, just three years after graduating from the Nova Scotia College of Art and Design. In 1959 he entered the Benedictine Monastery in Weston Priory, Vermont, where this vase was made. His work owes its forms and spiritual sense to Song Dynasty Chinese pottery and other classic wares he admires and studies. His vessels are characterized by

an incredible range of form and color yet all are within a disciplined or basic order of variants. Forms of vessels are based on pure geometric shapes that suggest classic origins. He uses two metals for colors: copper and iron. Both form and color evolve separately as he does not throw pots to match glazes or make glazes to fit pots. Both are developed independently for their beauty. "They are related, not by conscious planning, but by interior intuition."[2]

Brother Thomas uses technical skill as the means to share his spiritual view of work. He feels an urgency that is not completed with throwing, glazing and firing. The completion comes about when he is able to share his message with others, a mutual recognition of the beautiful. He comments that those who see beyond the vessel comprehend the artist's vision and know it somehow as their own: "To see beyond the work is the essence of every great work of art."[3]
J.L.F.

1. In 1982 eight pieces were bequested to the Museum by Donald O. Reichert who held the first major retrospective of works by Brother Thomas in Springfield in 1980. See: Donald O. Reichert, *Ceramics of Weston Priory/Brother Thomas* (Springfield, Massachusetts: The George Walter Vincent Smith Art Museum, 1980). In 1984 *Wintermoon* (1984.445), a Brother Thomas vase with iridescent pearl white glaze, was purchased by staff and friends in memory of the late Mary Quinn, a department assistant overcome with cancer.

2. Brother Thomas (Thomas Bezanson), *The Studio Potter*, vol. 14, no. 2, p. 62. See also *The Porcelain of Brother Thomas* (Boston, Mass: David R. Godine in association with Pucker Safrai Gallery, Boston, 1987).

3. *Ibid.*

Peter Voulkos (b. 1924)

46.
Untitled (exh. no. 109)
Berkeley, California, about 1959-1960
Glazed stoneware with epoxy paint
H. 27½ in., w. 12½ in., D. 6¼ in.

Signed in black slip near base: Voulkos
Anonymous Gift 1979.502

Inspired by the excitement and spontaneity of Abstract Expressionist painting and sculpture, American ceramicists of the 1950s broke away from European and Oriental traditions and challenged the utilitarian vessel form. The leader of this transformation was Peter Voulkos.[1] Before 1955, when Voulkos was invited to teach ceramics at Black Mountain College, near Asheville, North Carolina, he had worked in a relatively conventional manner, producing utilitarian wares. While teaching at Black Mountain, Voulkos visited New York and met such premier Abstract Expressionists as Franz Kline, Willem de Kooning, and David Smith. He was captivated by the freedom and energy of their work and their commitment to share ideas with one another. The following four years were the most productive and exciting years of Voulkos's career.

Voulkos incorporated challenging combinations of form and bold brush strokes, expressing the energies of Abstract Expressionism three-dimensionally by slashing and erupting the surfaces of his vessels. He stacked cylinders, spheres, and discs, joining them together on a cylindrical base to form

an assemblage. Like the work shown here, the sculptures were typically massive, monolithic, and bulging volumes with an energized surface that was brilliantly colored in areas. At a time when many ceramicists were trying to imitate oriental glaze effects, Voulkos introduced epoxy paints in 1958. Through such bright sculptural work and hundreds of workshop demonstrations he conducted throughout the country, Voulkos dramatically influenced ceramics students in American university art programs.
M.P.

1. Garth Clark, *American Ceramics 1876 to the Present*, (New York: Abbeville Press, 1987), p. 99. Rose Slivka, "The New Ceramic Presence," *Craft Horizons*, vol. 21, no. 4 (July/August 1961), pp. 30-37. For information on Voulkos and his style, see Rose Slivka, *Peter Voulkos: A Dialogue with Clay*, (New York: Little, Brown and Company, 1978).

Wayne Higby
(b. 1943)

47.
Mirage Lake (exh. no. 116)
Alfred, New York, 1984
Raku-fired earthenware
H. 11⅛ in., DIAM. (rim) 18½ in., DIAM. (base) 5¾ in.

Stamped: 84
Gift of Mary-Louise Meyer in Memory of Norman Meyer 1984.770

In the early 1970s, many American ceramicists developed interest in *trompe l'oeil* effects. Taking inspiration from the Surrealists, ceramicists transformed clay into the guise of numerous other surfaces, including cardboard, leather, wood, and paper. In a similar vein, the vessel surfaces of works like Wayne Higby's *Mirage Lake* are transformed into rocky landscape formations.

Higby developed an interest in ceramics in the mid 1960s during a six-month world tour, when he encountered Minoan and Islamic ceramics. The former revealed the possibility of metaphors in a vessel while the latter emphasized the relationship between form and decoration. During his childhood in Colorado, Higby was profoundly influenced by the magnificent rocky land formations of the Grand Canyon, and he has incorporated these images into his work.

Since 1973, Higby has been a professor of ceramics at the New York State College of Ceramics in Alfred, New York, where he has demonstrated and argued for the integration of function and meaning in vessels. His work has developed from hand-built coiled pots to wheel-thrown bowls such as *Mirage Lake*. Using a rubber-resist method of applying glazes and raku-firing, he creates wonderful crackle-glazed surfaces and landscape images. Higby typically concentrates on two forms: a tall oval bowl and a conjoined group of lidded vessels. He decorates the outer and inner surfaces of his vessels with precision, uniting foreground and background to form a continuous landscape of valleys, lakes and canyons.[1]
M.P.

1. For Higby biography and discussion of style and period, see Louise Klemperer, "Wayne Higby," *American Ceramics*, vol. 3, no. 4, pp. 32-37 and Susan Wechsler, *Low-Fire Ceramics*, (New York: Watson-Guptill Publications, 1981), pp. 82-87. Wayne Higby, "Comment," *American Craft*, vol. 49, no. 1 (February/March 1989), pp. 16-17; and Garth Clark, *American Ceramics 1876 to the Present*, (New York: Abbeville Press, 1987), pp. 141-177 and 273.

METALS

John Coney
(1655/56-1722)

48.
Baptismal Basin (exh. no. 26)
Boston, Massachusetts, about 1718
Silver
H. 3¼ in., D. 17 in.

Marked on bottom: crowned "IC" over coney within shield
Gift of a Friend of the Department and Edward J. and Mary S. Holmes Fund 1984.208

John Burt
(1692/93-1745/46)

Pair of Flagons
Boston, Massachusetts, about 1722
Silver
H. 14³⁄₁₆ in., w. 9½ in.

Marked on body to left of handle thumbpiece: crowned "IB" above a pellet in a shield
Gift of a Friend of the Department and Edward J. and Mary S. Holmes Fund 1984.204, 205

In 1906 the Museum mounted the first exhibition devoted exclusively to silver in a major American museum. Many Massachusetts churches loaned their plate to this pioneering show of American colonial silver, and to a subsequent one on ecclesiastical silver held in 1911. After the second exhibition some churches left their silver on loan, while others bequeathed their silver to the Museum. The Brattle Street Church gave fourteen monumental pieces in 1913.[1]

The Unitarian Universalist Church of Marblehead (formerly the Second Congregational Society) was among the many Massachusetts churches to loan silver for the 1911 exhibition. The silver remained on loan to the Museum, escaping the fire that destroyed the meeting house in 1912. Facing financial difficulties in the early 1980s, the church offered the Museum the opportunity to purchase its exceptional service, which included four beakers, three tankards, two flagons, a basin, a dish, and a spoon. Most of the silver bears the inscription "to Mr. Holyoke's Church" and dates from the years 1716 to 1728.

With Edward Holyoke as its minister, the Second Congregational Society was founded in 1717 by a group of prosperous newcomers from Boston, Salem, and England, in reaction to the conservative, locally-dominated First Society.[2] The liberal theology and cosmopolitan views of the church members are reflected in its silver service, which includes two pairs of egalitarian and domestic beakers, along with its two examples of the flagon – a purely ecclesiastical form. Prominent inscriptions that honor the minister also reflect the hierarchical structure of the Anglican church.
E.S.C.

1. Francis Hill Bigelow, *Historic Silver of the Colonies and Its Makers* (New York: The Macmillan Company, 1917).

2. The best discussion of Marblehead's religious institutions is Christine L. Heyrman, *Commerce and Culture: The Maritime Communities of Colonial Massachusetts, 1690-1750* (New York: W.W. Norton, 1984), esp. 273-303. The meaning of forms and inscriptions on church silver is discussed by Barbara M. Ward, "'In a Feasting Posture': Communion Vessels and Community Values in Seventeenth-and Eighteenth-Century New England," *Winterthur Portfolio* 23, no. 1 (Spring 1988), pp. 1-24.

Richard Conyers
(about 1668-1708)

49.
Tankard (exh. no. 22)
Boston, Massachusetts, 1697-1708
Silver
H. 5 in., W. 5 ½ in., D. 3 ⅞ in.

Marked to right of handle and on top of lid:
"RC," below a crown, within a shield
Gift of Stuart Alan Goldman and Marian E.
Davis Fund 1980.278

Richard Conyers, a freeman in the Guild of
London Goldsmiths, probably arrived in Boston in about 1697, and died there in 1708.[1]
The fact that so few examples of Conyers's
work are known is partly due to his short career in Boston, but also suggests the difficulties
for newcomers establishing their own shop in
the well-knit Boston community. Conyers's
1701 imprisonment for debt implies that such
immigrants, despite their training, probably
lacked the network of patronage that was
necessary to support themselves.[2] The initials
"T R I" engraved on the bottom of the tankard may someday provide information about
Conyers's patrons.[3]

To date, fewer than ten works in silver having a Conyers mark have been identified, of
which this diminutive tankard is the latest discovery. Its unusual size in combination with
such finely finished details as the gadrooned
lid, crenate lip, scrolled thumbpiece, fine cast
cherub's mask terminal and deeply defined
base molding distinguish the tankard as one
of the finest examples of Conyers's work.
Conyers and David Jesse, another London-trained silversmith who arrived in Boston at
the end of the seventeenth century, apparently
introduced such fashionable English details as
cut-card ornament and gadrooning to the
flourishing Boston trade.[4]
J.J.F.

1. Barbara McLean Ward, "The Craftsman in a
Changing Society: Boston Goldsmiths, 1690-1730"
(Ph.D. diss. Boston University 1983), p. 350.

2. Transcription of imprisonment document, Suffolk
Court of Common Pleas 1699-1701, p. 136. Conyers file, Bigelow-Phillips files, Yale University Art
Gallery.

3. Thomas and J. Redmond have been suggested as
the likely owners of the Conyers tankard. Conyers
file, Bigelow-Phillips files, Yale University Art Gallery, np.

4. Ward 1983, p. 160.

John Coney
(1655/56-1722)

50.
Punch Bowl (exh. no. 25)
Boston, Massachusetts, about 1710
Silver
H. 5 in., D. 9 ⅝ in.

Marked on bottom: crowned "IC" set over
coney within shield
Theodora Wilbour Fund in Memory of Charlotte Beebe Wilbour 1972.913

The establishment of a new, more restrictive
charter in 1692, with its provision for English
officials and political appointees, placed Boston
and Massachusetts under stricter English political and economic dominion. A growing
number of locals sought to benefit from the
external encroachment of the royal system by
establishing and maintaining English ties and
standards. Increases in the migration of English craftsmen, the importation of goods, the
quantity of specie, and mercantile opportunities resulted in a flourishing of production in
architecture and decorative arts.[1]

John Coney was Boston's leading silversmith from 1690 to 1720, earning commissions from government, colleges, and
churches. The large number of surviving objects and the stylistic variety of his marked
work reflects a productive shop able to adjust
to changes in fashion. The key to this flexibility was his ability to hire skilled journeymen
or pieceworkers, some of whom had recently
arrived from England.[2] While most of Coney's known work was in the more baroque
style learned from his master Jeremiah Dum-

mer, this punch bowl is distinguished by its
strong, contained shape and plain surface. It
is the earliest known monumental piece of
Georgian silver made in Boston. Engraved
with the Riddell coat of arms, the punch bowl
was purchased by Walter Riddell (d. 1738), a
very successful commodore in the British
navy stationed in Boston between 1708 and
1710.[3] Riddell took the bowl with him when
he returned to England, where it remained
until it was sold at auction in 1971. The architectural emphasis on form, the plain treatment of the surface, and the crest contrast
with the more elaborate forms, repoussé decoration, and floral engraving of the previous
twenty years. Like the Warland chest of about
1715 (see exh. no. 24), the Riddell punch
bowl demonstrates a second wave of Anglicization in the second decade of the eighteenth
century. Purchased by a British mariner from
a leading Boston craftsman, its provenance
and stylistic features reveal the closer cultural
ties of the period.
E.S.C.

1. On the relationship between changes in the socio-political structure and the material culture, see
Benno Forman, "Urban Aspects of Massachusetts
Furniture in the Late Seventeenth Century," in John
Morse, ed., *Country Cabinetwork and Simple City
Furniture* (Charlottesville: University Press of Virginia, 1970), pp. 1-33; Barbara M. Ward, "The
Craftsman in a Changing Society: Boston Goldsmiths, 1690-1730," (Ph.D. diss., Boston University, 1983); and Edward S. Cooke, Jr., "The Warland Chest: Early Georgian Furniture in Boston,"
Maine Antique Digest (March 1987), section C, pp.
10-13.

2. For a discussion of Coney's productive success,
see Ward. An older catalogue of his works is Hermann Clarke, *John Coney, Silversmith, 1655-1722*
(Boston: Houghton Mifflin Company, 1932).

3. G. T. Ridlow, *History of the Ancient Ryedales*
(Manchester, NH: published by the author, 1884),
p. 87.

John Coney
(1665/6-1722)

51.
Chocolate Pot (exh. no. 27)
Boston, Massachusetts, 1710-1722
Silver, wood
H. 9⁷⁄₁₆ in., DIAM. (base) 4⁷⁄₁₆ in.

Marked on bezel, near lid, above spout, and
on bottom: crowned "IC" over coney within
shield
Partial gift of Dr. Lamar Soutter, Theodora
Wilbour Fund in memory of Charlotte Beebe
Wilbour, and the Marion E. Davis Fund
1976.771

This magnificent chocolate pot indicates an
era of high prosperity for colonial merchants
and silversmiths alike in Boston in the late
seventeenth and early eighteenth centuries.
The continuous influx of foreign-trained silversmiths at the turn of the century combined
with the increased wealth and aspirations of
prominent Boston citizens to stimulate production of innovative forms and styles. In the
late seventeenth century, the practices of
drinking hot chocolate from the West Indies,
coffee from the Americas, and tea from the Far
East were introduced which further inspired
the production of new forms. Master silversmith John Coney, like his contemporaries,
employed English-trained journeymen or
pieceworkers in his shop who provided designs for these newly popular forms. While
the majority of late seventeenth-century master silversmiths enjoyed high social status and
active public service, Coney, son of a Boston
artisan, concentrated his attentions on his
silversmithing profession serving as the pre-
eminent silversmith of the early eighteenth
century.[1]

This chocolate pot, one of the earliest of its
form, shows the fine craftsmanship of Coney's
shop, and great sensitivity to design which included the popular serpent headed spout
motif.[2]

The original coat of arms engraved on the
pot were erased and replaced by the initials of
later owners William Downes and Elizabeth
Edwards Cheevers, probably at the time of
their marriage in 1749.
R.J.M.

1. Barbara McLean Ward, "The Craftsman in a
Changing Society: Boston Goldsmiths, 1690-1730,"
(PhD diss., Boston University, 1983).

2. Two other early chocolate pots exist in public
collections, one at the Museum of Fine Arts, and
one at the Metropolitan Museum of Art in New
York. The addition of a second removable finial
such as the one Coney added to the lid of this pot
(later soldered in place) enabled the insertion of an
implement for stirring up the chocolate.

Jacob Hurd
(1702/3-1798)

52.
Teakettle-on-Stand (exh. no. 29)
Boston, Massachusetts, 1730-1740
Silver
H. 14³⁄₈ in., D. 7½ in.

Marked on lid: "HURD" in ellipse; marked on
later burner: "N. HARDING & CO/BOSTON/
coin"
Gift of Esther Lowell Abbott in memory of
her mother, Esther Lowell Cunningham,
Granddaughter of Jarves Russell Lowell
1971.341

The teakettle-on-stand is an exceptional example of the equipment associated with the
newly fashionable consumption of tea at social gatherings in the first half of the eighteenth century.[1] Comparable in quality and
style to the finest works produced by contemporary English silversmiths, it is one of few
colonial New England silver pieces of this
form and size. Numerous brass kettles and
their stands from the mid-eighteenth century
survive, indicating the popularity of this form
in the base metals.[2] Physical evidence indicates that many of these pieces were silvered
originally, a less expensive alternative to the
solid silver form. The nearly sixty ounces of
silver comprising this kettle and stand would
have fashioned three or four contemporary
teapots. The engraved arms, skillfully executed by Hurd, attest to the status of its owners. The Reverend John Lowell, the first minister of the Newburyport church at the age of
twenty-two, drew on his grandmother's family
crest – the three passant dolphins of the
Leversedge arms – to quarter the Lowell
arms. To this crest the liberal and said to be
sometimes impulsive minister added his own
motto: "Occasionem Cognosce" (trans.
"Know the moment").
R.J.M.

1. See Rodris Roth, "Tea Drinking in 18th-Century
America," *U.S. National Museum Bulletin* NO225
III, Paper 14, (Washington, D.C.: Smithsonian Stud-
ies in History and Technology, 1961), pp. 63-91.
See also Kathryn C. Buhler, *American Silver in the
Museum of Fine Arts Boston, 1655-1825* (Boston:
Museum of Fine Arts, 1972), pp. 642-644.

2. Rupert Gentle and Rachael Feild, *English Domestic Brass, 1680-1810* (New York: E.P. Dutton &
Co., Inc., 1975), pp. 159-161.

Jacob Hurd
(1702/3-1758)

53.
Small-Sword with Scabbard and Waistbelt with Frog (exh. no. 30)
Boston, Massachusetts, 1735
Silver, steel, leather
L. 30½ in.

Marked on shell of hilt: "HURD" in ellipse
Gift of Jane Bortman Larus in honor of
Kathryn C. Buhler and in recognition of her
warm friendship and association with Mark
Bortman and Jane B. Larus 1984.109

Marked, American-made swords from the colonial era are quite rare, and only the exceptional sword is inscribed and retains its original fittings. This sword by Jacob Hurd is
engraved with the name of Colonel Richard
Hazen, and the date it was fashioned along
with its original cost. It is still housed in its
original leather scabbard, waistbelt, and
frog.[1] While Hurd fashioned the silver hilt
and mounts, like many American sword makers, he may have relied upon foreign imports
for his forged steel blades, and probably employed local craftsmen to make the leather fittings. A lethal, if decorative, means of gentle-
manly self-defense, this small-sword was
likely used for dress occasions, which undoubtedly has contributed to its survival.

Jacob Hurd was better known as a silversmith and engraver of domestic and ecclesiastical silver than as a maker of swords for New
England's elite. Among the nine known surviving swords with Hurd's mark are one made
for Colonel William Prescott (1726-1795),
who commanded the American forces at the
Battle of Bunker Hill, and another for General John Winslow (1703-1774), grandson of
Governor Josiah Winslow.[2] Colonel Richard
Hazen (1696-1754), the original owner of the
Museum's sword, was a Harvard graduate
who was born in Haverhill and became a sur-
veyor. Hazen established the line of demarca-
tion between Massachusetts and New Hampshire in 1741, and was an extensive land-
owner in Penacook, now Concord, New
Hampshire.[3]

J.J.F.

1. Engraved on guard of hilt: R. H. 1735. Engraved
on scabbard fitting: R. Hazen of Haverhill A.D.
1735 Cost £ 13 = 15 = 9.

2. See Bowdoin College Museum of Art, "The Win-
slows," p. 17 for a brief biography of John Winslow
and his painting by Joseph Blackburn.

3. Clifford K. Shipton, *Sibley's Harvard Graduates*
(Boston: Massachusetts Historical Society, 1942),
vol. 6, pp. 186-189.

Benjamin Burt
(1729-1805)

Engraving by Nathaniel Hurd
(1729/30-1777)

54.
Teapot (exh. no. 35)
Boston, 1763
Silver with ebonized wooden handle
H. 5⁷⁄₁₆ in., w. 9¼ in., D. 4¼ in.

Marked on bottom: "BENJAMIN / BURT" in
cartouche
Gift of Jane Bortman Larus in honor of Mrs.
Llora Bortman 1985.16

Rococo-style silver holloware with magnificent floral repoussé-chased ornamentation
characterizes the most advanced level of Boston metalsmithing of the 1760s and 1770s.
The high standard of workmanship of Boston
silversmiths was known throughout New England. Even cosmopolitan individuals from
such prosperous towns as Hartford and Newport regularly purchased silver from Boston
silversmiths. Such patronage is exemplified by
this Benjamin Burt teapot, commissioned as
part of a larger service by Providence merchant Moses Brown and his cousin Ann
Brown upon their marriage in 1763.

Brown's commission was inspired by a sim-
ilarly chased service given to Ann Brown's
older sister Sarah upon her 1762 marriage to
Providence lawyer Jabez Bowen.[1] On both
surviving teapots the engraving indicates that
the sisters' father, Obadiah Brown, paid for
them, yet surviving correspondence indicates
that Moses played an active role in the com-
missioning of the Brown service.[2]

Correspondence from Moses Brown to
Benjamin Burt reveals the close interaction
between patron and craftsman and points to
the specialization of particular skills among
the highly developed Boston silversmith community. Brown wished to have the service
"made in the Neatest Manner in yᵉ same
fashion of those you Lately made for Mr. Ja-

bez Bowen." As Brown requested, the teapot shows the same expert but unidentified hand at work in the repoussé decoration that encircles the shoulder of the teapot as found in the 1762 Bowen teapot. Brown also requested the engraving of family arms "the same as that Mr. N. Hurd Ingravd on a Seal for me Some time past."[3] Nathaniel Hurd was perhaps the best engraver in mid-eighteenth century Boston, as demonstrated by his many surviving bookplates, seals, and documents. Hurd frequently engraved silver holloware, using Guillim's *A Display of Heraldry* to familiarize himself with the needed coat of arms.[4]

J.J.F.

1. A teapot from the Bowen service is in the Museum's collection, 1983.210. Both services are treated in Robert P. Emlen, "Wedding silver for the Browns: A Rhode Island family patronizes a Boston goldsmith," *American Art Journal*, vol. 16., no. 2 (Spring 1984), 39-50. Emlen speculates that the Bowen teapot was part of a larger wedding service.

2. The initials "O = B" as found in "O = B to S = B" on the Bowen teapot, and "O = B to A = B" as found on the Brown's teapot, are for Obadiah Brown, who gave these gifts to his daughters Sarah and Ann.

3. Correspondence dated 19 August 1763 and 2 September 1763, Moses Brown Papers, Manuscript Collection, Rhode Island Historical Society, as quoted in Emlen, pp. 41, 43.

4. Hurd's portrait by John Singleton Copley (Cleveland Museum of Art) shows the sitter with his 1724 copy of Guillim's compendium of armorial design. Jules David Prown, *John Singleton Copley in America 1738-1774* (Cambridge, Mass.: Harvard University Press, 1966) vol. 1, plate 177.

Paul Revere
(1735-1818)

55.
Tankard (exh. no. 36)
Boston, Massachusetts, 1768
Silver
H. 9¼ in., w. 7 in., D. 5 in.

Marked to left of handle: "REVERE," in rectangle
Gift of Edward N. Lamson, Barbara T. Lamson, Edward F. Lamson, Howard J. Lamson and Susan L. Strickler 1986.678

Presentation silver, used in religious ceremonies or to commemorate important individuals or events, were the most prestigious commissions of early Boston silversmiths.[1] The American tradition of tutorial silver began at Harvard in 1695. Students demonstrated their appreciation for their tutor by presenting a piece of silver such as a porringer, cann, salver or tankard. Stephen Scales was a tutor at Harvard College during the tumultuous years of the late 1760s.[2] Gifts of tutorial silver declined during these years; however,

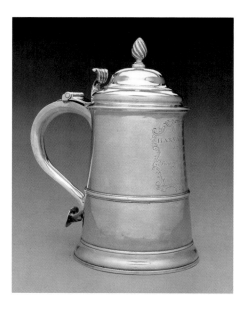

before leaving in 1770 to practice law in New Hampshire, Scales received a silver cann and this silver tankard made and engraved by Paul Revere II.

The decoration on both the tankard and the cann symbolize a dramatic restructuring of the curriculum instituted by Harvard president Edward Holyoke (1689-1769) in 1767. Tutors, previously responsible for the students' entire curriculum, were now assigned to one of four specialties: Latin; Greek; natural philosophy, mathematics and geography; and logic, metaphysics and ethics.[3] Scales's assignment to this last field is represented by two books engraved at the top of the cartouche, "Price's Mor." (symbolizing Richard Price's "Review of the Principle Questions in Morals," 1758) and "Locke's essay" (symbolizing Thomas Locke's "Essay Concerning Human Understanding," 1690, adapted 1743). Both were required reading among a range of ethics texts.[4]

R.J.M.

1. See Michael K. Brown's essay, "The Colonial Period" in *Marks of Achievement: American Presentation Silver* (Houston: Museum of Fine Arts, 1987), pp. 23-73. See also the entries for silver in the catalog, *Harvard Tercentenary Exhibition* (Cambridge, Mass: Harvard University Press, 1936) pp. 19-44.

2. For a discussion of Harvard student life during these years see Sheldon Cohen's articles in *New England Quarterly* 97 (1974) and *Colonial Society of Massachusetts*, vol. 59.

3. Samuel Eliot Morison, *Three Centuries of Harvard 1636-1936* (Cambridge, Mass.: Harvard University Press, 1936), p. 90.

4. Information on Harvard curriculum provided by Thomas J. Siegel, Lecturer in History and Literature, Harvard University, see also Thomas J. Siegel, "Governance and Curriculum at Harvard College in the Eighteenth Century" (PhD diss., Harvard University, 1990).

56.
Mourning Pin (exh. no. 46)
Boston, Massachusetts, 1787
Gold frame with glass cover, plaited hair
H. 1⅞ in., w. 1⅛ in.
Gift of Mr. Charles H. Wood 1985.1027

Mourning Pendant
Boston, Massachusetts, 1787
Gold frame with glass cover, ivory with water color and gold thread, plaited hair on reverse
H. 1⅞ in., w. 1⅛ in.
Gift of Mr. Charles Wood 1985.1025

In seventeenth-century New England, mourning rings, gloves, handkerchiefs and bottles of wine and rum were distributed at funerals as gifts to the friends and relatives of the deceased.[1] Originating from a European tradition dating to the Middle Ages, American mourning rings were usually engraved with the name, date of death, and age of the deceased. In the late seventeenth and much of the eighteenth centuries, many of these gold rings were engraved or chased with the iconography of death – winged death's heads, skeletons, coffins and skulls. Toward the end of the eighteenth century, rings, necklaces, bracelets, pins and pendants for mourning use were made in an increasing variety of materials, including hair, enameled ivory, and seed pearls. Changing religious attitudes towards death – from the pessimism of the Puritans to more optimistic attitudes following the Great Awakening – made the morbid symbolism of earlier rings unfashionable. Such neoclassical motifs as urns, plinths, and mourners in flowing dress became common on increasingly larger forms of jewelry. These images were commonly set in an enclosed garden with a willow, reflecting the popularity of the new rural cemeteries at the end of the eighteenth century. Romantic inscriptions were often engraved or painted into the decoration.[2] The decorated ivory was then framed to form rings and pins. In the case of the mourning pendant, two metal strips were affixed to either side of the frame to which eight strings of beads would have been attached to form a choker.

The mourning pin with plaited hair reflects a concurrent fashion in mourning jewelry. Hair, commonly imported from France, was used in framed ovals or woven into multiple patterns of braids to form necklaces and bracelets.[3] Since this pin has plaits of hair on both sides of its body, with the reverse oval of a different color hair, it is possible that the piece was a stock item that was subsequently individualized by the addition of braided hair, probably of the deceased, to the back.

R.J.M.

1. For a further discussion of American mourning practices see Anita Schorsch, *Mourning Becomes America: Mourning Art in the New Nation* (Clinton, N.J.: The Main Street Press, 1976), and Rachel J. Monfredo, "American Finger Rings Representing Bonds of Relationships" (Master's thesis, University of Delaware, 1990).

2. Painted on the pendant's obelisk is the poesy: GO/SPOTLESS/INNOCENCE/TO/ENDLESS/BLISS. Both the pendant and the pin commemorate the death of nine-year-old George Washington Hancock, son of Massachusetts' first govenor and famed patriot, John Hancock (1737-1793). Each piece is engraved on the reverse: In (Memory) o(f) Geo. Washington Hancock/ obt. 27. Jan. 1787. AEt. 9. Yrs.

3. See Mark Campbell, *The Art of Hair Work: Hair Braiding and Jewelry of Sentiment with Catalog of Hair Jewelry* (Originally published in 1875. Reprint, Berkeley, Calif: Lacis Publications, 1989).

Higbie and Crosby
(active 1825-1830)

57.
Tea Service (exh. no. 51)
New York, New York, 1825-30
Silver

Teapot: H. 10¼ in., W. 12 in., D. 5 in.; marked: "HIGBIE & CROSBY / (face in profile) (crowned head) C (star)." Covered sugar bowl: H. 9¾ in., W. 9½ in. D. 4¾ in.; marked: "(face in profile) (crowned head) C (star) / HIGBIE & CROSBY." Creamer: H. 8 in., W. 7 in., D. 3¾ in. Marked: "(face in profile) (crowned head) C (star)."
Gift of Dr. and Mrs. Roger G. Gerry
1975.649-651

The neoclassically refined forms and simple geometry that were characteristic of all the decorative arts during the late eighteenth and early nineteenth centuries gave way to a bolder and more robust expression in the 1820s. Holloware dating from this period consisted of thin rolled sheet silver, hammered into complex, rotund shapes, often accentuated with pronounced lobes and usually dominated by a reliance on milled and cast decoration.

Ransom Crosby and Aaron H. Higbie were working in New York when it became America's largest city and port. They were listed as jewelers in *Longworth's New York Directory* from 1825 to 1832, after which time Higbie may have left the partnership.[1] The broad-hipped, lobed body and the densely packed floral decoration of the Higbie and Crosbie tea service represents the technological aesthetic of the day that combined the traditional repoussé of thin sheet silver embellished with innovative milled bands.[2]
J.J.F.

1. Higbie and Crosby were originally attributed to the Boston area by Stephen G.C. Ensko, *American Silversmiths and their Marks II* (New York: Robert Ensko Incorporated 1937), p. 40. Wendy Cooper reattributed the silversmiths to New York when this service was acquired by the Museum. Dorothy E. Ellesin, ed., "Collector's Notes" *Antiques* vol. 110 November 1976, p. 936.

2. The technological advances that made milled banding possible also enabled some silversmiths to sell these elements to other makers. A die-rolled grapevine ornament made by Moritz Furst (b. 1792) of Philadelphia was used by Nicholas Bogert of Newburg, New York, in an 1835 tea service, as seen in lot number 71 in the 23 January 1988 Christie's New York sale.

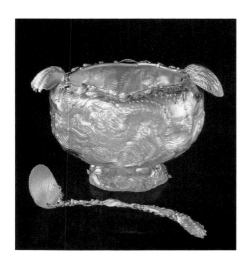

Gorham Manufacturing Company
(1831-)

58.
Punch Bowl and Ladle (exh. no. 70)
Providence, Rhode Island, 1885
Silver
Bowl: H. 10⅛ in., D. 15¾ in.; marked on bottom: "(lion) (anchor) G / (wolf's head) /1980 / STERLING." Ladle: L. 14 in.; marked: "STERLING"
Edwin E. Jack Fund 1980.383, 384

During the 1870s and 1880s, American metalsmiths derived many decorative and technical ideas from non-Western cultures, particularly Japan. The "opening" of Japan by Commodore Perry in 1854 brought metalwares and woodblock prints that inspired a dominant decorative style in the West. These designs and the imitation of Japanese metal combinations to generate different colors of metals were incorporated into Western forms, creating an Anglo-Japanese aesthetic.[1]

Metal was the medium that most readily incorporated this Japanese influence. Such firms as Gorham and Tiffany had been producing metal holloware with chinoiserie decorative motifs including dragons, pagodas, willows, and fretwork since the 1850s.[2] By the late 1860s, distinctively Anglo-Japanese designs appeared, integrating motifs of bamboo shoots, insects, birds, and sea life. The style was further popularized by a furnishings display at the Philadelphia Centennial Exhibition of 1876. Sea motifs associated with the Japanese aesthetic were common by the 1870s and 1880s.

This monumental punchbowl, datemarked 1885, displays an extravagant use of realistic images of ocean life. Attention to anatomical accuracy is reflected in the numerous species of cast crabs, seaweed, and shells attached to both the ladle and the bowl. The overall decoration progresses from the ocean bottom and

its associated sea life at the bowl's base, to the seaside of sand, crabs, shells and washed-up seaweed at the bowl's upper lip. Crustaceans, seaweed, cattails and sand decorate the ladle.

Unfortunately, the records at Gorham are incomplete, and the original owner's name as well as any record of additional objects purchased with the punch bowl have been lost. In an era of increasing machine-manufactured silver, the extravagant, hand-wrought ornament suggests this was a display piece, intended to indicate its owner's fashionable taste and wealth.
R.J.M.

1. See Charles H. Carpenter, Jr. and Janet Zapata, *The Silver of Tiffany & Co. 1850-1987* (Boston: Museum of Fine Arts, 1987). See also David A. Hanks with Jennifer Toher, "Metalwork: An Eclectic Aesthetic" in *In Pursuit of Beauty: Americans and the Aesthetic Movement* (New York: The Metropolitan Museum of Art, 1987), pp. 252-293.

2. Charles Carpenter, *Gorham Silver* (New York: Dodd, Mead, and Co., 1982), pp. 94-120.

Gorham Manufacturing Company
(1831-)

59.
Pitcher (exh. no. 71)
Providence, Rhode Island, about 1885
Silver
H. 10 in., W. 7¼ in., D. 4½ in.

Marked on bottom: "(lion) G (within an escutcheon) (anchor); STERLING; 1295; (boar's head)"
Edwin E. Jack Fund 1983.331

Fueled by archeological excavation and a quest for new experiences, a taste for the exotic was notable throughout Western culture in the late nineteenth century. One aspect of this interest was the Egyptian revival, which included a romantic rediscovery of Cleopatra and the circumstances of her death by a poisonous snake. The reptilian imagery so popular in the literature and visual arts of this period is powerfully depicted in this sinuous snake pitcher.

In the 1880s, Gorham Manufacturing Company developed a line of wares marked by experimentation with imaginative forms that included *trompe-l'oeil* "napkins" in plates, "silk shawls" wrapped around pitchers, and applied, three-dimensional floral and vegetal elements made to scale.[1] Remarkable for the unsettling realism of its two entwining snakes, this pitcher is a *tour de force* of repoussé chasing. Although the identity of the designer and silversmith remains unknown, this masterfully executed pitcher attests to the technical and artistic prowess of the craftspeople employed by the Providence firm.
J.J.F.

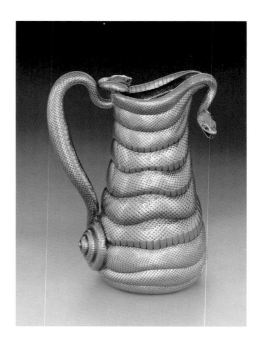

1. Charles H. Carpenter, Jr., *Gorham Silver 1831-1981*, (New York: Dodd, Mead & Company, 1982), pp. 117-118, 129.

Arthur J. Stone
(1847-1938)

60.
Jardiniere (exh. no. 82)
Gardner, Massachusetts, about 1902
Copper with silver details
H. 5 in., D. (rim) 7½ in.

Marked on bottom: Stone (with hammer crossing the "t")
Gift of Alma Bent 1987.464

The Arts and Crafts movement of the late nineteenth century promoted handcraftsmanship, honest use of local materials, and the worker's continual involvement in the design and production of a piece.[1] Silver, copper, brass and other base metals, which had previously been accorded different levels of prestige, were all deemed worthy of fine workmanship. The 1882 Gorham Manufacturing Company catalog advertised a line of copper wares introduced in 1881, as "choice examples of an art kindred to that of precious metals."[2] While the production of copper wares at Gorham ended in 1885, copper production was revived in places like the Roycroft Copper Shop in East Aurora, New York, during the Arts and Crafts movement.

As the movement grew in America, it enhanced the appreciation of decorative, utilitarian objects or the "applied arts." The 1904 Universal Exposition of Saint Louis, Missouri (the Louisiana Purchase exposition) was the first American event that displayed the applied arts along with painting, sculpture and architecture – the traditional fine arts – instead of with the manufactured goods. Arthur Stone exhibited a small group of metalworks in the exhibition, including this jardiniere, for which he received a silver medal.

One of the preeminent silversmiths in America, Stone trained under Edwin Eagle in Sheffield, England, and emigrated to the United States in 1884 to work for the William B. Durgin Company in Concord, New Hampshire. He later opened his own shop in Gardner, Massachusetts, and showed his silver work extensively at the Boston Society of Arts and Crafts. The Museum owns an extensive collection of Stone silver, the core of Stone's library, and several of his copper vessels. Stone's copper work is quite rare since he made copper pieces for his own use, rather than for sale. Yet, his work in the base metal demonstrates the same design sensitivity and technical execution of his work in silver. The fine repoussé and chasing delineating the oak leaves around the graceful curve of this jardiniere is among Stone's finest work in any metal.

R.J.M.

1. For a complete discussion of the Arts and Crafts movement, see Wendy Kaplan's *"The Art That is Life"*: *The Arts and Crafts Movement in America, 1875-1920* (Boston: Museum of Fine Arts, 1987), for discussion of the jardiniere, see pp. 281-282. The jardiniere was given to the Museum in appreciation of the exhibit accompanying this book.

2. Charles Carpenter, Jr., *Gorham Silver 1831-1981* (New York: Dodd, Mead and Company, 1982), p. 112.

George C. Gebelein
(1878-1945)

61.
Coffee and Tea Service (exh. no. 84)
Boston, Massachusetts, 1929
Silver

Tea kettle on stand: H. 12¼ in., w. 9 in.; marked on base: "GEBELEIN (in rectangle) / STERLING / Boston." Coffee pot: H. 8¾ in., w. 9½ in.; marked on base: "Gebelein (in keyhole cartouche)/ STERLING / Boston." Teapot: H. 8¾ in., w. 9½ in.; marked on base: "Gebelein (in a keyhole cartouche) / STERLING / Boston." Creamer: H. 6¼ in., w. 4⅝ in.; marked on base: "Gebelein" (in keyhole cartouche), "STERLING", and "Boston." Covered sugar bowl: H. 8½ in., w. 3¾ in.; marked on base: "Gebelein" (in keyhole cartouche), "STERLING" , and "Boston."
Anonymous Gift 1986.778-782

In the late nineteenth century, interest in colonial artifacts and their styles increased dramatically due to nationalistic fervor and the Arts and Crafts movement's emphasis on preindustrial craft technologies and indigenous expression. Many designers and craftspeople began to draw more consciously from the past. Boston became one of the centers of colonial-revival work, and George C. Gebelein established himself as the most important and skilled silversmith to work in that style.[1]

Gebelein learned silversmithing as an apprentice in the Boston firm of Goodnow and Jenks, where he learned older handraising and decorating techniques as well as newer machine techniques. His training there also

linked him, in his mind, to Paul Revere; he believed he could trace his apprenticeship lineage back through preceeding masters to the patriot silversmith. After completing his apprenticeship Gebelein gained additional knowledge as a journeyman for Tiffany & Co. of New York and William B. Durgin and Company of Concord, New Hampshire. He learned as much as possible from the commercial silver world, but became increasingly aware of the attention given to antique silver by museums and periodicals that glorified the work of past craftsmen. Drawn by the tenets of the Arts and Crafts reformers, Gebelein joined the cooperative Handicraft Shop of the Boston Society of Arts and Crafts in the fall of 1903. He prospered in an environment that emphasized historical roots and quality craftsmanship and eventually opened up his own shop in 1909 at 79 Chestnut Street in Boston. Inspired by the attention to craftsmanship, strength of form, and purity of line found on American colonial silver, Gebelein developed his own interpretation of historical work, yet also collected, sold, and repaired the authentic plate.[2]

This set, a wedding present of 1929, demonstrates Gebelein's artistic indebtedness to colonial silversmiths, particularly Paul Revere, to whom Gebelein felt so spiritually and aesthetically linked. The set closely resembles a covered sugar bowl (35.1759) that Revere made for his own family's use. From the bowl, Gebelein borrowed the fluted urn-shaped body; the raised, domed foot set upon square plinth; the brite-cut swag and border engraving; and the flame finial. Even the elliptical cartouche for the owner's monogram on the Gebelein service is based upon the Revere original. However, Gebelein fashioned his own expression by using the same fluted urn body shape for all the pieces in the service. While Revere made services comprised of a fluted elliptical teapot, fluted urn sugar bowl, and smooth helmet-shaped creamer, Gebelein made all the pieces match. He also added a new form – the tea kettle on stand. In addition his work reveals more robust lines and deeper engraving.

E.S.C.

1. The best summary of this period is Wendy Kaplan, ed., *"The Art that is Life": The Arts & Crafts Movement in America, 1875-1920* (Boston: Museum of Fine Arts, 1987), esp. pp. 170-181.

2. Biographical information drawn from Margaretha Gebelein Leighton, *George Christian Gebelein, Boston Silversmith, 1878-1945* (Lunenburg, Vermont: Stinehour Press, 1976).

Josephine Hartwell Shaw
(active about 1900-1935)

62.
Necklace (exh. no. 85)
Boston, about 1915
Gold, glass, jade
L. 20 in.

Marked on applied tab: "J. H. SHAW"
Gift of Mrs. Atherton Loring 1984.947

In the late nineteenth century, Boston became a center for design and craftsmanship inspired by Asian and colonial precedents. The trustees and staff of the Museum of Fine Arts and the Massachusetts Normal Art School and the members of the Boston Society of Arts and Crafts, often working together, served as a catalyst for collecting and producing high-quality decorative arts. In terms of numbers of craftsmen and numbers of objects shown or sold, metalworking, which included jewelry, was the largest branch of the Society.[1]

Josephine Hartwell Shaw, who was educated at Massachusetts Normal Art School and Pratt Institute, became one of the leading metalworkers in the Boston area. She displayed her work at numerous shows, including the 1911 exhibition of contemporary crafts at the Museum of Fine Arts. After a second show at the Museum in 1913, a necklace and brooch made by Shaw were given to the Museum. Even though women comprised the vast majority of the Society's membership, Shaw was one of the few women on its male, architect-dominated governing board. As a member of the Society, she worked closely with Frederic Allen Whiting, the chairman of the jewelry department, who encouraged craftspeople to draw inspiration from primitive cultures and from oriental, Egyptian, and Greek work. Shaw's necklace for her neighbor Atherton Loring demonstrates this interest in oriental style and materials, even incorporating eighteenth-century western Chinese white jade plaques. The necklace itself, worked on the front and back like the jade, demonstrates the maker's skill with color and texture. The emerald-colored glass, greenish gold and white jade complement each other; and the glass rectangles provide regular rhythm between the chain of rods, loops, and balls. As a beautiful example of the time-consuming, intricate work performed by a skilled craftsperson who was not dependent on her craftwork for her living, the necklace provides valuable insight into the local craft community in the early twentieth century.[2]

E.S.C.

1. On the environment in Boston, see Beverly Brandt, "Mutually Helpful Relations: Architects, Craftsmen and the Society of Arts and Crafts, Boston, 1897-1917" (Ph.D. diss., Boston University, 1985).

2. For information on Shaw, see Wendy Kaplan, ed., *"The Art that is Life": The Arts & Crafts Movement in America, 1875-1920* (Boston: Museum of Fine Arts, Boston, 1987), pp. 267-268.

Margret Craver
(b. 1907)

63.
Teapot (exh. no. 91)
Wichita, Kansas, about 1936
Silver and Gabon ebony
H. 5½ in., w. 9½, D. 5 in.

Mark on base: "C (within a stylized six-petaled flower)"
Gift in Memory of Joyce Goldberg with funds provided by Mr. John P. Axelrod, Mr. and Mrs. Sidney Stoneman, Mr. Charles Devens, Mr. and Mrs. Peter S. Lynch, The Seminarians, Mr. James G. Hinckle, Jr., The MFA Council, and Friends 1988.533

In the early twentieth century, technical advances in spinning and stamping silver fostered assembly-line practices that nearly extinguished traditional methods of hand raising silver. Despite a brilliant but short-lived revival during the Arts and Crafts movement, only a few isolated silversmiths were still at work in the mid-1920s.

Margret Craver, who decided upon a career as a silversmith several years before her graduation in 1929 from the University of Kansas, found the decline of the craft particularly distressing. Since there was little formal schooling in metals, she learned her craft by studying privately with the few practicing silversmiths she could find: Wilson Weir of Tiffany's; Stone Associates in Gardner, Massachusetts; Arthur Nevill Kirk, a former instructor at Cranbrook; and Leonard Heinrich, chief armor conservator of The Metropolitan Museum. Craver completed her education with a trip to Europe in 1938, where she studied with Baron Erik Fleming, Silversmith to the King of Sweden. Craver returned to the United States during the war, and worked with Handy and Harman, a leading refiner of precious metals, to develop therapeutic metalsmithing projects for returning veterans and later to train design teachers in the craft.[1] As part of this effort, Craver ran five National Silversmithing Workshop Conferences between 1947 and 1959. These conferences had an overwhelming impact on the direction of contemporary American metalsmithing, as most artists working today were either trained during the conference, or learned from a silversmith who was a participant. Craver's own training and teaching provided a link between the silversmiths of the early twentieth century and those craftsmen-designers who began to mature in the 1950s.

This silver teapot was the first major work in holloware conceived and raised by Craver. Her absorption of Art Deco form is evident in the teapot's profile, yet its underlying organic volume reveals its affinity with the pre-war era. Craver's work has a timeless quality that comes from her original sense of design and her willingness to experiment with the un-known. Margret Craver's life-long dedication to merging traditional techniques and con-temporary expression and her zeal for teach-ing and sharing her insights places her among the first rank of American goldsmiths and jewelers.[2]

J.J.F.

1. Margret Craver, "The Handy and Harman Con-ferences" unpublished manuscript, 24 September 1982.

2. Craver's awards include fellowship in the Ameri-can Crafts Council, its Gold Medal for Excellence, and membership in the Master Gold and Silver-smiths Guild of Sweden.

Maria Regnier
(b. 1901)

64.

Tea Service (exh. no. 92)
Saint Louis, Missouri, 1939
Silver, ivory
Teapot: H. 6 in., W. 11¾ in., D. 6 in.; marked: "MR / STERLING / HAND WROUGHT." Creamer: H. 2¼ in., W. 6¾ in., D. 3⅜ in.; marked: "MR / STERLING / HAND WROUGHT." Covered sugar bowl: H. 2¾ in., W. 4½ in., D. 3½ in.; marked: MR / STERLING / HAND WROUGHT

Gift of John E. Goodman 1989.60-2

Born in Hungary in 1901, convent-educated Maria Regnier moved at the age of twenty with her family to the United States and set-tled in Saint Louis, Missouri. She explored the arts in nearly all media throughout her youth, and embraced her métier upon attending her first metalworking class in 1934 at Washing-ton University, one of the few institutions to offer instruction in metalsmithing at the time. Regnier continued her education at the Rhode Island School of Design in Providence and the Dixon School in New York. Following her studies, she taught metalsmithing to the deaf.

Maria Regnier's sure sense of geometric de-sign and natural abilities brought her quick recognition.[1] She actively exhibited her work to popular acclaim and received commissions from such luxury stores as Gump's, Nieman-Marcus and Marshall Field. During wartime Regnier applied her metalsmithing skills to airplane construction for the government.

The service was Regnier's first fully realized work in holloware. Although its simple, streamlined design is related to art deco, tech-nically there is nothing of the machine age about Regnier's work. Regnier hand-raised and planished the unusually heavy gauge metal, to create "jewel-like facets."[2] The qui-etly reflecting silver of this buoyant oval ser-vice demonstrates Regnier's singular mastery of her medium.

J.J.F.

1. Regnier's work was reviewed in numerous news-papers in St. Louis, Missouri, Savannah, Georgia, and New York City. Newspaper clippings, depart-mental artist files.

2. Regnier's one-woman exhibition at the Leah K. Curtiss Gallery, 460 Park Avenue was reviewed in the *New York Times* on 16 March 1950.

Albert Paley
(b. 1944)

65.
Plant Stand (exh. no. 120)
Rochester, New York, 1988-89
Mild steel; brass, slate
H. 56 1/2 in., w. (max.) 25 1/2 in.
Marked on base: "© PALEY STUDIOS LTD.
1988"

Purchased through funds provided by The
National Endowment for the Arts and The
Seminarians 1989.78

The accomplishments and energy of Albert
Paley have ushered in the current renaissance
in architectural metalwork in America. During the first third of the twentieth century,
hand-forged ironwork in both historical and
contemporary styles adorned many struc-
tures. American ornamental metalworkers,
led by Frank and Gustav Koralewsky of Boston, Samuel Yellin of Philadelphia, and Wil-
helm Hunt Diederich gained international
acclaim for their architectural work. Unfortunately, the Depression and the military demands on metalworkers during World War II
brought this ornamental iron industry to an
end.[1]

A graduate of the Tyler School of Art in
Philadelphia, Paley established himself as a
jeweler making rings, brooches, and pendants
in a very organic, curvilinear style. Inspired
by his experience forging steel, his appreciation of early twentieth-century metalwork,
and his belief that traditional techniques
could give modern buildings the human value
and tactile warmth they often lacked, Paley
entered and won the 1972 competition to design and build the gates for the newly reno-
vated Renwick Gallery of the Smithsonian Institution. Since turning from jewelry to
metalwork, Paley has received a Fulbright Fellowship, several NEA grants, and an award
from the American Institute of Architects. His
work is in the permanent collections of the
Metropolitan Museum of Art, Philadelphia
Museum of Art, and Virginia Museum of
Arts, among others.[2]

Paley's work will never be misunderstood
as historical reproduction. His interest in
composition and attention to detail have produced a new artistic expression. Exploiting

the plasticity of the material and the strength
and permanence of the final product, Paley
takes full advantage of new technology, using
electric arc welders and hydraulic presses to
rephrase the base metal.

The organic plant-like rods that curve and
twist around the MFA's forged and fabricated
plant stand are Paley's signature; he twists the
steel with a machine of his own invention,
adapted from an elevator motor. This plant
stand is a pivotal small-scale work. Paley had
previously made a number of steel plant
stands, but for this commission he added
brass detailing and the wavy steel ribbon mo-

tif, first used on the large sculptural fixtures at
the Wortham Center in Houston, Texas. The
stand thus incorporates Paley's personal
small-scale work and the best of his new
large-scale architectural work.

E.S.C.

1. On American ornamental ironwork, see Wendy
Kaplan, ed. *"The Art that is Life": The Arts &
Crafts Movement in America, 1875-1920* (Boston:
Museum of Fine Arts, Boston, 1987), pp. 137-138.
2. The best summary of Paley's career is *Albert
Paley: The Art of Metal* (Springfield, Massachu-
setts: Museum of Fine Arts, 1985).

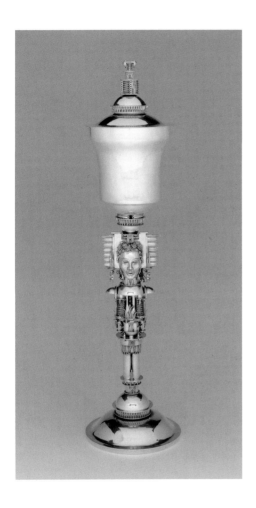

Richard Mawdsley
(b. 1945)

66.
Standing Cup (exh. no. 121)
Carterville, Illinois, 1986
Silver
H. 17⅜ in., D. (base) 4¼ in.

Marked on base: "RM STERLING SN / AG"
Anonymous Gift 1988.535

Silver holloware, which entails time-consuming skilled workmanship, has not been a prominent part of American decorative art production in the past thirty years. Although such metalsmiths as Jack Prip, Hans Christensen, and Olaf Skoogfors provided a strong foundation in design and fabrication for the increasing number of college students majoring in metalwork during the 1950s and 1960s, holloware is not emphasized in current metal curriculums. Because the costs of materials and tools for small ornaments are less than those for vessels, most graduates of artisanry or design programs focus upon jewelry production. Those who do make holloware often use base metals such as brass, pewter, or iron. Richard Mawdsley is one of a small number of metalworkers to produce silver holloware as well as small-scale jewelry.

Mawdsley is best known for jewelry that combines mechanically-inspired imagery with labor-intensive fabrication and manipulation of precious materials. Mechanical imagery has been an essential part of his compositions since his undergraduate studies at Kansas State Teacher's College. Mawdsley's work at that time consisted of single-piece castings of such industrial parts as cogs, gears, or rods. While a graduate student at the University of Kansas at Lawrence, he developed an interest in the toy-like whimsies of the blacksmith Brent Kington and the fastidious detailing of the jeweler John Paul Miller. Metal tubing serves as both structure and embellishment in Mawdsley's jewelry of the 1970s and 1980s, which successfully blends mechanical details, playful imagery, and technical virtuosity. By using them for anatomical or naturalistic compositions, Mawdsley plays with the industrial character of the parts, further transforming them into one-of-a-kind precious objects. The resulting objects possess a distinctive historical symbolism.[1]

Mawdsley has taught metalsmithing with Kington at Southern Illinois University, Carbondale since 1978. He works at a methodical pace, making two or three pieces a year. The standing cup is his best piece of holloware, demonstrating an aesthetic coherence and technical refinement lacking in his earlier work. The traditional ecclesiastical form integrates a raised cup, tubularly constructed body and headdress, and repoussé face with wild hollow wire hair to create a multilayered sense of ritualistic imagery. Mawdsley succeeds in creating a new context for human figure and machinery within a liturgical context.

E.S.C.

1. The best reviews of Mawdsley's career are *Richard Mawdsley: Master Metalsmith* (Memphis: National Ornamental Metal Museum, 1987); and Janet Koplas, "Richard Mawdsley's Tubular Fantasies," *American Craft* 43, no. 2 (April/May 1983), pp. 18-21.

Charles Crowley
(b. 1958)

67.
Tea Service on Stand (exh. no. 122)
Waltham, Massachusetts, 1987
Silver, cast aluminum; enamel paint
H. 30 in., L. 19 in., W. 16 in.

Signed on the bottom of all three vessels:
"Charlie Crowley / 1987"
Gift of Ronald and Anne Abramson
1987.232

Most advocates for American crafts in the
1950s and 1960s extolled the virtues of handcrafted fabrication. Metalworkers eschewed
the use of such industrial equipment as lathes
and milling machines, favoring instead ham-
mers and stakes for raising and shaping and
traditional solder joints. Due to the lasting
legacy of the Arts and Crafts movement, there
was an emphasis on process as the sole crite-
rion of quality. Handcrafted was inherently
better than manufactured. Only recently have
craftspeople and advocates of the crafts taken
a less deterministic view and recognized that
the skill of the maker is in choosing the appropriate means to achieve the desired result.[1]

Of contemporary metalsmiths, Charles
Crowley is one of the leaders in this new ac-
ceptance of machinery. Crowley, a graduate
of Boston University's Program in Artisanry,
has developed a personal style that stems
from his interest in and knowledge of milling
machines and lathes. He conceives his designs
with his machinery in mind and refines his
ideas by quickly working test pieces on his
machines. The speed and precision of his
equipment enable him to explore, change,
and refine without losing his inspiration. After working the forms up on the machines,
Crowley then uses a more traditional and
time consuming approach to detailing and
finishing. His finished products thus combine
a very modern feeling with meticulous detailing. Crowley has focused almost exclusively
on holloware, although during the past five
years his interest in making woodworking
joints in metal with milling machines has led
him to fabricate several tables and chairs. In
his recent services he has chosen to make inte-
grally designed stands rather than trays.[2]

This particular tea service manifests the
clean, machined lines sought by Crowley as
well as his interest in building a sympathetic
stage for the service. He spun the silver coni-
cal forms on a lathe, then milled an aluminum
table frame. The shape of the vessels and the
finned applications to the vessels and table
create an illusion of speed and sleekness, but
Crowley tempered this modernist emphasis
with the softness of the curved lines in the
teapot handle, the thumbpieces of the lids,
and the cylindrical spouts. Automobile enamel sprayed on the cast and joined aluminum parts offsetsthe potential coldness of the
sleek lines. Crowley's sense of detail is also
well illustrated by the sugar bowl, the

"spout" of which is actually a cylindrical handle for a detachable sugar spoon. The service
thus combines Crowley's interest in simple,
machine-generated geometric forms with expressive details.

E.S.C.

1. The influence of the Arts and Crafts rhetoric and
the importance of appropriate use of free or regu-
lated work is explained in David Pye, *The Nature
and Art of Workmanship* (London: Cambridge University Press, 1968).

2. For a brief biography of Crowley, see *American
Craft* 48, no. 2 (April/May 1988), pp. 56-57.

South Boston Flint Glass Works
(1812-1827) or

Phoenix Glass Works
(1819/20-1870)

68.
Decanter (exh. no. 56)
Attributed to Thomas Cains
(1779-1865)
South Boston, Massachusetts, 1813-1835
Free-blown colorless flint glass
H. 10½ in., w. 5¼ in.

The William H. Fenn III Glass Collection
1978.698

During the late eighteenth and early nineteenth centuries, most glass blowers in America were foreign-born and foreign-trained. To meet the demand for European glass wares, American factories employed European craftsmen to imitate high-quality wares and patterns. The Embargo of 1807, as well as the War of 1812, which interrupted the importation of foreign wares, further stimulated the need for domestically produced glass wares.[1]

The Boston Glass Manufacturing was established in 1787 to produce thin crown glass to compete with imports from Bristol, England. Superintendent Charles F. Kupfer sailed to England in 1811 to enlist glassblowers experienced in Bristol methods. Upon his return, however, a wartime blockade prevented the importation of special sands needed to produce crown glass. The company therefore established a new factory, The South Boston Flint Glass Works, to produce domestic flint glass wares under the direction of Thomas Cains, an expert glass blower from Bristol.[2]

Cains has been traditionally credited as the father of the New England flint glass industry. Born in Gloucester County, England, Cains was the son of a glassmaker, and apprenticed at the Phoenix Glass Works in Bristol. He immigrated to the United States in 1812 and worked as a glassblower at the South Boston Flint Glass Works. In charge of production, Cains remained there until about 1819 or 1820 when he established his own glass factory, the Phoenix Glass Works. The glass wares produced by Cains typically incorporated applied triple bands around the body or cover, bands of chain decoration, and hollow-

knopped stems or covers containing a coin. The ribbed decoration and chain decoration used by Cains was probably in imitation of some of the late eighteenth-century English glass wares. Decanters of Cains's 1813-1835 period were usually decorated with either single or triple ring decoration and a blown hollow stopper with a "mercurial" ring around its largest diameter.[3] One of several Cains pieces and about 650 other pieces of nineteenth-century glass in the William H. Fenn III Glass Collection, this decanter features two bands of applied chain decoration and two single bands around its neck; unfortunately, the stopper is not original.
M.P.

1. See Arlene Palmer Schwind, "The Glassmakers of Early America," *The Craftsman in Early America*, (New York: W.W. Norton & Company, 1984) pp. 158-189 and George S. and Helen McKearin, *American Glass* (New York: Crown Publishers, 1941) pp. 132-137, 242-244.

2. See Lura Woodside Watkins, "Glassmaking in South Boston," *Antiques*, September 1945, pp. 140-143 for establishment of the South Boston Flint Glass Works.

3. For information on Cains, see Kenneth M. Wilson, *New England Glass and Glassmaking*, (New York: Thomas Y. Crowell Company, 1972), pp. 197-228.

New England Glass Company
(1818-1888)

69.
Covered Jar (exh. no. 67)
Engraved by Louis Friedrich Vaupel (1824-1903)
East Cambridge, Massachusetts, about 1875
Colorless lead glass
H. 4⅝ in., W. 3 in., D. 3 in.

Gift of Mrs. Mildred M. March 1976.633

The New England Glass Company of Cambridge, Massachusetts, was renowned for its high-quality lead glass, and won many awards in its early years for its cut, stained, and pressed glass and paperweights. The firm's most celebrated works were those engraved between 1853 and 1885 by Louis Vaupel, one of the best foreign-born engravers of the period.[1]

The son of a German glassmaker, Vaupel grew up with the craft, assisting in all phases of glassmaking and decoration. Glass engraving was a highly developed skill among the Bohemian glassmakers, and it became Vaupel's specialty. When the German economy slumped at mid-century, Vaupel sought employment in the United States, where he was hired by New England Glass Company. He became superintendent of the highly regarded engraving department and decorated all of the works displayed by the company at the Philadelphia Centennial Exhibition of 1876.[2]

The lack of signatures on most works executed in glass factories makes it difficult to ascertain an individual hand at work. However, this covered jar and several other examples in the Museum's collection bear family monograms and have descended directly through succeeding generations of the Vaupel family.[3] The jar features the initials "MN," referring to the artist's daughter, Minette Vaupel Newman, and typifies Vaupel's unusually fine workmanship. It is engraved with flowers on each of its four sides. The delicate rendering of ferns, thistles, tulips, roses, and chrysanthemums demonstrates the artist's close observation of nature. The decoration and unusual form illustrate the skill of the engraver and the range of the New England Glass Company.

J.J.F.

1. The pioneering study of the New England Glass Company is Lura Woodside Watkins, *Cambridge Glass 1818 to 1888, The Story of the New England Glass Company*, (Boston: Marshall Jones Company, 1930). See also Kenneth M. Wilson, *New England Glass and Glassmaking* (New York: Thomas Y. Crowell Company, 1972), pp. 229-61.
2. Carl U. Fauster, "Louis Vaupel, master glass engraver," *Antiques* (May 1971), 696-701.
3. Objects in the Museum's collection are: goblet, 61.1219; goblet 61.1222; sugar bowl, 61.1223; standing cup, 61.1224; standing cup, 61.1225; spoon holder, 1976.729.

Steuben Division of Corning Glass
(1918-)

70.
Intarsia Vase (exh. no. 95)
Frederick Carder (1863-1963)
Corning, New York, 1920-about 1930
Blown, triple-layered colorless and black glass
H. 8¾ in., DIAM. 3½ in.

Facsimile inscription engraved on lower lobe of vessel in script: "Fred'k Carder"
Gift of Prof. Emeritus F. H. Norton and the Department of Metallurgy and Materials Science, Massachusetts Institute of Technology 1971.592

Free-blown glass vessels with floral and animal decoration in the Art Nouveau style were popular both here and abroad in the late nineteenth and early twentieth centuries. In the United States, the demand for this glass was met primarily by Tiffany Studios and by Steuben Glass Works (1903-1917).

Frederick Carder, the founder of Steuben Glass Works, had been a designer and decorator at the Stourbridge, England, glassmaking firm of Stevens and Williams. Carder came to Corning, New York, to produce blanks for T. G. Hawkes and Company, a glass engraving factory. In Corning, Carder also experimented with his own lines, the first of which was the shimmering metallic luster glass that he called Aurene. Over Carder's long career, he revived numerous lost glassmaking techniques and introduced many new ones. He considered intarsia glass, named for its visual similarity to *tarsia*, the Italian term for inlay work in all media, to be his greatest effort.[1]

To create intarsia glass, sheets of crystal and colored glass were plated together. After an acid-resist design was painted on the colored glass, an acid bath left the desired pattern in relief. Another layer of colorless glass was added, sandwiching the colored glass between two sheets of crystal, and the whole was then carefully blown into a vessel without distorting the design. Carder personally etched the design for each of the works, while the glassblower fashioned the object.[2] Fewer than one hundred examples of intarsia glass are known today, each of them unique. The difficulty of the technique and the onset of the Great Depression undoubtedly curtailed further production of this labor-intensive, expensive item.

J.J.F.

1. The standard reference on Carder is Paul V. Gardner, *The Glass of Frederick Carder* (New York: Crown Publishers, Inc., 1971), pp. 3-31.
2. Albert Christian Revi, *American Art Nouveau Glass* (Nashville, Tenn.: Thomas Nelson, Inc., 1968), p. 171-72. According to Revi, Swedish-born John Jenson, said to be Carder's most trusted glassblower, may have made intarsia glass. Gardner 1971, 73-75.

John La Farge
(1835-1910)

71. (color plate)
Morning Glories (exh. no. 73)
Six-paneled window from William Watts
Sherman House, Newport, Rhode Island
Boston, Massachusetts, 1877-78
Leaded stained glass
H. 86½ in., w. 72 in.

Gift of James F. and Jean Baer O'Gorman
1974.498

The wide ranging artistic contributions of
John La Farge, neglected for most of this century, have received a favorable reappraisal in
recent years.[1] His innovative efforts with
stained glass inspired a lively era of experimentation in this medium. La Farge eschewed
the popular medieval and ecclesiastical styles
of the period and sought to achieve three-dimensional pictorial effects through the use of
opalescent glass rather than such commercial
techniques as enamels, paints, or stains.[2] Until his death, La Farge continued to experiment with stained glass and natural stones of
all thicknesses, textures and shapes, so as to
breathe translucency and depth into this
medium.

La Farge was already an established water-
colorist, oil painter, and a fine designer, when
at mid-life he drew upon his remarkable sense
of color to explore stained glass. His 1876
mural decoration for Trinity Church designed
by architect Henry Hobson Richardson led to
one of La Farge's first commissions in stained
glass for Richardson's next project, the William Watts Sherman house in Newport,
Rhode Island. Their collaboration produced
one of the earliest domestic settings in which
stained glass appeared as a fully conceived element of the architectural plan.

The six-paneled window that La Farge designed was probably made by Page, McDon-
ald and McPherson of Boston.[3] La Farge employed the rich colors of English medieval
pot-metal glass with some painting and cross-
hatching, but added a delicate counterpoint in
the subtly modulating translucency of white
opalescent glass flowers. A "japonaise" trellis
motif employed in the design made use of
lead lines and flattened the window format
even while it allowed the morning glories to
expand in space. The result was a significant
break from medieval or commercial traditions
in motif and technique.
J.J.F.

1. See the exhibition catalogue on the artist by
Henry Adams et. al., *John La Farge* (New York: Abbeville Press, 1987).

2. La Farge applied for a patent for the use of opalescent glass in stained glass windows in 1879,
which he received in 1880. Tiffany was experi-

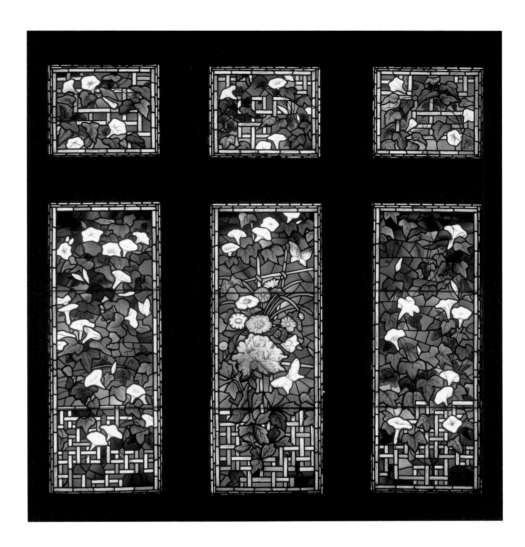

menting with the material at the same time, but re-
ceived his patent one year later. Dianne H. Pilgrim
"Decorative Art: The Domestic Environment" in
The American Renaissance 1876-1917 (New York:
Pantheon Books, 1979), p. 131.

3. McPherson's name appears in a letter from La
Farge to Sherman, cited by H. Barbara Weinberg
The Decorative Work of John La Farge (New York:
Garland Publishing Inc., 1977), p. 349, fn. 2. A re-
lated watercolor in the Museum's collection is prob-
ably an early study for the transom lights (11.2826).
See also Jane S. Becker, cat. no. 1, in Wendy Kaplan,
*"The Art that is Life": The Arts & Crafts Move-
ment in America, 1875-1920* (Boston: Museum of
Fine Arts, 1986) p. 62; Doreen Bolger Burke et al.,
*In Pursuit of Beauty, Americans and the Aesthetic
Movement* (New York: Rizzoli, 1986), pp. 185-88,
447-449; Howard John Iber, in Robert Judson
Clark, ed., *The Arts and Crafts Movement in Amer-
ica 1876-1916* (Princeton, N.J.: Princeton Univer-
sity Press, 1972) p. 18.

4. Other stained glass in the Museum's collection by
La Farge include *Peonies Blown in the Wind*
(13.2802), *The Infant Bacchus* (23.249), *Butterflies
and Foliage* (38.954), *Fish and Flowering Branch*
(69.1224).

Kreg Kallenberger
(b. 1950)

72.
View from Saddleback Ridge from the Osage
Series (exh. no. 117)
Tulsa, Oklahoma, 1990
Cast optical crystal, cut, polished, sand-
blasted, and oil stained
H. 7⅜ in., w. 19½ in., D. 5½ in.

Signed on bottom proper right: "KK"
This project was supported in part by a grant
from the National Endowment for the Arts, a
Federal agency, and The Seminarians
1990.122

In the early 1960s Dominick Labino (1910-
1987) invented a portable fire-brick furnace
and annealing oven. While working molten
glass had traditionally been an industrial en-
deavor, this invention prompted Harvey Littleton (b. 1922), professor of ceramics at the
University of Wisconsin, to explore the possibilities for artists to make and blow molten

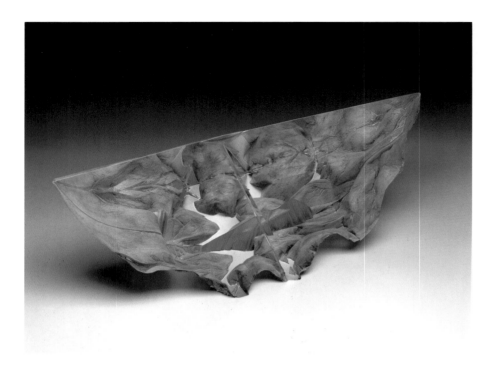

glass in their own studios. The success of these Toledo Workshops, held in 1962, led to Littleton's establishment of a glass program at the University of Wisconsin, and encouraged many of his students to establish glass studios and programs at other universities as well. By the mid-1970s technical knowledge was widely available, and glass artists were concentrating on ideas rather than techniques.[1]

Born in Austin, Texas, Kreg Kallenberger studied ceramics at the University of Tulsa in Oklahoma during the early 1970s, where he helped to establish a glass studio. Like Littleton and his followers, he became intrigued with the form, light, and texture of glass, and turned from ceramics to glass.

View from Saddleback Ridge is a remarkable example from the Osage series, which was inspired by the landscape near Kallenberger's home in the foothills of the Ozark Mountains in Osage County. Although Kallenberger admires the expansive rocky land formations of Albert Bierstadt's paintings, the mystical views of this series are not real but imaginary.[2] They change as the viewer moves around the piece, actively engaging the viewer.

M.P.

1. Factual information gleaned from Susanne K. Frantz, *Contemporary Glass: A World Survey from The Corning Museum of Glass* (New York: Harry N. Abrams, Inc., 1989) and Dan Klein, *Glass: A Contemporary Art*, (New York: Rizzoli International Publications, Inc., 1989).

2. Author's conversation with Kreg Kallenberger, February 14, 1990.

Dan Dailey
(b. 1947)

73. (color plate)
"Dense Growth" Vase from the Science Fiction Series (exh. no. 118)
Blown in Williamstown, West Virginia and decorated in Amesbury, Massachusetts, 1984-1986
Glass and fired glass enamels
H. 11½ in., DIAM. 10 in.

Signed on vessel side just above base: "Dailey;" signed on bottom: "SF-4-84 / DENSE GROWTH"
Gift of Mr. and Mrs. John S. Clarkeson
1987.571

Studio glass, like studio furniture and ceramics, is in the midst of a period of vitality, fueled by an interest in the past combined with a self-conscious expression of contemporary ideas. Unlike the pioneering studio glassmakers of the 1960s and 1970s, who restricted themselves to working alone and using the techniques associated with small-studio work, today's glassmakers blend the efficiency of multiple series characteristic of traditional factory glassmaking with more individualistic possibilities. One of the masters of this new studio glass is Dan Dailey. As a designer, he has worked for such factories as Daum, Fenton, and Steuben; as a teacher he is co-director of the glass program at the Massachusetts College of Art and has taught at Pilchuck School and Haystack Mountain School of Crafts; and as an artist he has shown his work at galleries and museums throughout America and

abroad. For Dailey, materials and techniques of its fabrication are not the basis of inspiration even though his technical skill is superb. Rather Dailey generates his ideas through constant sketching of characters, animals, commentary, or situations in a fanciful or abstract way. He then applies these drawings to a variety of glass media: vessels, wall reliefs, lamps, cast-block walls, or constructed sculptures. In spite of this versatility, it is the vessel form that ultimately intrigues Dailey.[1]

Dailey's Science Fiction series is his most successful venture in the vessel form. Each of the vessels in this limited edition of twenty features different body colors and different stylized decoration of animal or humanoid forms. He blew the vessels at the Fenton Company, a glass factory in West Virginia, and decorated them at his studio in Massachusetts. He masked out the vessel design, sandblasted it for the desired relief depth, unmasked it and lightly sandblasted the entire surface for an even finish, and then acid-polished the whole vase. Finally he stippled the background of the relief with opaque glass enamels. The resulting vessel has many levels of complexity and mystery: the deep cobalt blue color of the body with the contrasting copper green rim, the abstract fantasy figures of the relief design, the rhythms of the stippling, and the overall satin finish that is impervious to fingerprints.

E.S.C.

1. The best summary of Dailey's career is *Dan Dailey: Simple Complexities in Drawings and Glass, 1972-1987* (Philadelphia: Philadelphia College of Art, 1987).

Hohokam
(300 B.C. - A.D. 1450)

74.
Bowl (exh. no. 1)
Colonial Period, Santa Cruz Phase
Arizona, Gila or Salt Rivers, A.D. 700 - 900
Red-on-buff earthenware
H: 3¾ in., DIAM. 10½ in.

Gift of Mr. and Mrs. Peter S. Lynch, Anne and Joseph P. Pellegrino, Anonymous Gift, and Frank B. Bemis Fund 1989.235

The prehistoric desert farmers identified as the Hohokam settled in small cooperative groups along the Gila and Salt rivers in the Sonora Desert of Arizona as early as 300 B.C. Evidence suggests the Hohokam were immigrants from Mesoamerica who brought with them a fundamental understanding of water management and pottery making. This bowl was made during the florescence of the Hohokam culture. This era saw great achievement not only in art but in the development of sophisticated desert irrigation systems, communal architecture, and a complex ceremonial calendar. Hohokam pottery of this period reveals an expressive and meaningful character differentiated from Mesoamerica origins. Although the Hohokam civilization came to an abrupt end around A.D. 1450, its influences can still be recognized in the cultural patterns and objects of present-day Pueblo people.

The flying bird image is a hallmark of the Hohokam culture. Development of the flying bird image can be traced alongside of the civilization's growth and decline. A selection of sherds from a Hohokam site occupied from the culture's nascency through its collapse makes clear that the notion behind the flying bird image was present from the formative stages. The image became fully realized and pervasive during the period of this bowl.[1]

The whirling image of a multitude of birds in flight poetically suggests a creation myth told in the Southwest, one that undoubtedly has been orally transmitted over several generations. It is said the World Creator received a drop of rain in his palm from which he made mud by mixing it with the earth. After fashioning a bird out of the mud the bird-form was transformed into a live flying bird. Thinking the bird needed companions, the Creator whirled the first bird rapidly around. The bird grew dizzy and saw many images of all species of birds — eagles, hawls and small birds. When the bird became himself the birds seen in his dizziness were in the world.[2]
L.L.F.

1. Emil W. Haury, *The Hohokam: Desert Farmers and Craftsmen, Snaketown, 1964-1965* (Tucson: University of Arizona Press, 1976. In collaboration with the Southwest Parks and Monuments Association).

2. Joseph Campbell, *Primitive Mythology, The Masks of God* (New York: Penguin Group, 1959), pp. 231-233.

Mogollon, Tularosa Phase

75.
Zoomorphic effigy (exh. no. 2)
Tularosa black-on-white
Near Reserve, New Mexico, A.D. 1100-1225
Gray earthenware, white and black slip
H. 10 in., W. 7½ in., D. 6¼ in.

Gift of a Friend of the Department of American Decorative Arts and Sculpture and Harriet Otis Cruft Fund 1989.316

The center of the prehistoric Mogollon culture roughly straddles the southern border of present-day Arizona and New Mexico. The Mogollon culture, like the Anasazi to the north and the Hohokam to the west, evolved from the seminomadic Cochise Desert culture, a group of hunters and gatherers who gradually developed an agricultural subsistence during the last five or six millennia B.C.

This rare effigy represents the late period of Mogollon cultural development, A.D. 1000-1400, when the pueblos were moderately large groups of rooms two and three stories in height. Late Mogollon sites disclose an unbridled complexity of ritual life, developed masonry skills and a variety of pottery types. In particular the pottery of this period indicates a cultural exchange and influence with the Anasazi who probably moved peacefully into the Reserve area as early as A.D. 1000 from the Zuni region. The mingling of cultures may have been responsible for the quickened cultural activity of this period.[1]

Archaeology of the last fifty years brings to light the beliefs revolving around the cycle of death and rebirth for these prehistoric people. The dead were nearly always buried in a flexed fetal position with their heads turned to the east, poignant symbols of rebirth. Effigies such as this are associated with burials of women and children. The effigies may be linked, in terms of property and symbol, with the matrilineal organization of the Southwest.[2] Few effigies have survived into the twentieth century, and this commanding figure is particularly noteworthy for its size and condition. Its multiple bird forms mark it as a sacred, unearthly being and suggest a correspondence to the following creation story told in the area today.

The Zunis believe that there are six directions rather than four: north, west, south, east, the zenith and the nadir. The zenith is composed of four ascending overworlds and the nadir of four descending underworlds. The world we know is the Middle. In the beginning, man began his growth and ascent from the womb of the furthest underworld, which was in total darkness. He ascended through the progressively lighter underworlds toward the Middle. In the underworld just below the Middle, which is spoken of as cave-like, the man-creature walked on all fours, had feet that were webbed like a duck, goggled eyes like those of an owl, ears like those of a cave-bat and, a bird-like tail. After the ascending journey, and upon emergence in the Middle, the creature stood upright and became man.[3]

L.L.F.

1. Paul S. Martin, *Prehistory: Mogollon. Handbook of North American Indians*, no. 9, Alfonson Ortiz, vol. ed. (Washington, Smithsonian, 1979), pp. 61-74.

2. Paul S., Martin, John B. Rinaldo, and Eloise R. Barter. "Late Mogollon Communities, Four Sites of the Tularosa Phase, Western New Mexico." *Fieldiana: Anthropology*, vol. 49, no. 1 (Chicago Natural History Museum, 1957).

3. Frank Hamilton Cushing, *Outlines of Zuni Creation Myths,* 13th Annual Report of the Bureau of American Ethnology (Washington, 1896).

Mimbres

76.
Bowl (exh. no. 3)
Classic, Style III, A.D. 1000-1150
Southwestern New Mexico
Earthenware; white and red to black slip
H. (uneven) 5⅛ in., DIAM. 11¼ in.

Seth K. Sweetser Fund and Gift of Supporters of The Department of American Decorative Arts and Sculpture 1990.248

The Mimbres group, part of the larger Mogollon culture, occupied a webwork of sites along the forty-six-mile north-south corridor of the Mimbres River Valley. While roughly contemporaneous to the Tularosa effigy (see cat. no. 2), this bowl, however, reflects a distinct Mimbres identity.[1] Mimbres potters produced beautiful geometric designs, and their painted representational images are unparalleled in all Southwest pottery. The poetically inspired painting on this particular bowl represents the Classic Style of Mimbres pottery.

This bowl, placed as a cap on the head of the deceased, may be seen as the dome of the universe. The painting, with its four-part division, suggests the four directions – north, west, south, east. The zenith and the nadir are indicated by the triangle pointing upwards and the central circular void. Perhaps most important, the kill, or central hole, allows spirit access to the underworld and overworld. The movement of the grand and whimsical bear-quail to the left around the Middle mimics the sinistral circuit, a beneficial, ceremonial course observed in Hopi ritual today.[2]

The ancient Mimbres were often buried in fetal position beneath the floors of their own homes. The burial context reflects the reverence for ancestors and symbolizes the belief in a life-death-life cycle. With this eloquent bowl and its dance of transformation the place of burial thus becomes the place of birth and emergence into another life.

L.L.F.

1. J.J. Brody's *Mimbres Painted Pottery* provides an excellent historical overview of the Mimbres culture that is attentive to the pottery paintings.

2. Jesse Walter Fewkes, *The Mimbres Art and Archaeology*, Essays between 1914 and 1924. Reprint (Albuquerque, New Mexico, Avanyu, 1989) Footnote, p. 36.

Acoma

77.
Olla (exh. no.6)
Acoma, New Mexico, about 1880
Earthenware; white, black and red slip
H. 11¾ in., DIAM. (max.) 10½ in.

Gift of Anne and Joseph P. Pellegrino
1988.290

This olla, a water jar, was made toward the end of the historic period, when the Southwest was opened by the coming of the railroads. It was a time of fascination with vast and strange landscape. Expeditions into frontier America were undertaken, artists and photographers sought out distant and grand vistas from which to work, and, for the privileged or determined, travel to the American west was the vogue. Along with the era's lively sense of adventure came the drive for collecting from faraway places. Acoma pottery was considered technically superior and was most prized by collectors. Between 1879 and 1885 the Smithsonian Institution collected more than 6,500 pottery objects from Zuni and Acoma alone.[1] The Indians of the Southwest were responsive to the demand, selling, directly and through traders, to the tourists and institutions. The provenance of this olla indicates that it was collected by photographer Alfred Wayland Cutting (b. 1860), from Wayland, Massachusetts, who traveled to Santa Fe in 1885.[2]

Acoma may be the oldest occupied settlement in North America. Old Acoma, or Sky City, sits on top of a sacred mesa with its nearby farming villages today situated near the mesa bottom. Only a few families and spiritual leaders live on the mesa top. However, the people maintain their ancestral homes and return to the mesa top for ceremonial days. While all of nature is held sacred, for the people of Acoma the three most important elements are earth, light and water. Water came only with the rain that filled the cisterns of Sky City. While women used to carry water in ollas on their heads from the cistern for daily use, the imagery and beauty of this olla express the reverential attitude toward collecting and storing water.

The minimal wear on this water jar indicates that it was carefully used, perhaps only for special occasions. The vessel is painted with rain symbols: steps or terraced shapes that refer to clouds. The triangular feather symbols might be described as the potter's prayers for rain so that the water jar will not be empty.[3]
L.L.F.

1. For a record of late nineteenth century collecting see Jonathan Batkin's *Pottery of the Pueblos of New Mexico 1700-1940* (Colorado Springs: The Taylor Museum of the Colorado Springs Fine Arts Center, 1987), pp. 137-139.

2. For more information see data folder in American Decorative Arts and Sculpture, Museum of Fine Arts, Boston.

3. For a record of symbols and interpretive remarks by Indians see Ruth L. Bunzel, *The Pueblo Potter*. Reprint: 1929 (New York: Dover Publishing Co.).

Attributed to Old Nampeyo of Hano (about 1850-1942)

78.
Bowl (exh. no. 9)
Hano, Arizona, about 1890
Sikyatki Revival
Earthenware; red and black slip
H. 4 in., DIAM. (max.) 13 in.

Gift of Laura F. Anderson 1984.626

The arrival of the Europeans in the Southwest around 1600 marked the beginning of the Historic Period, which continued through the opening of the frontier around the close of the nineteenth century. In late prehistoric years the Hopi of northeastern Arizona were making what many consider to be the most elegant and superb of Puebloan vessels, Sikyatki Polychrome, named after the archaeological site from which these extraordinary vessels were unearthed. Production of Sikyatki ware came to an end during the seventeenth century.

Nampeyo has been credited with the regenesis of Sikyaki ware. J. Walter Fewkes, project director of excavations at the Sikyatki site in 1895, writes of the "renaissance of old Sikyatki patterns under the lead of Nampeyo."[1] However, it is also thought that Thomas Keams promoted the revival of Sikyatki form and technique some years earlier. Shortly after the establishment of his Keams Canyon Trading Post in 1875, and certainly

by the early 1880s, Keams had asked unidentified Hopi potters to reproduce seven prehistoric vessels in the Sikyatki and San Bernardo
traditions.[2] However difficult it is to be certain
about who was first to advance the recovery
of this traditional style, it was Nampeyo's extraordinary creative skill and expressive sensibility that provided the real catalyst for the
Sikyatki revival.

When Indian potters use ancient sherds, as
Nampeyo did, they say they are "studying out
the line of the design." Pot and sherd side by
side clearly show that the ancient design has
been re-presented.[3] This bowl is replete with
rain imagery and might be thought of as
Nampeyo's prayer for rain. Hopi men planted
prayer feathers in supplication for rain, and
because women did not make prayer feathers,
they painted them on their pottery as a potent
visual entreaty for rain.[4] The central stylized
feather or wing symbol represents the thunderbird (see also cat. no. 11), a large bird
whose wings are said to sound like thunder,
a presage to a rainstorm.
L.L.F.

1. J. Walter Fewkes, "Designs on Prehistoric Hopi
Pottery," *Bureau of American Ethnology Annual
Report* 33, p. 212. See also Theodore R. Frisbie,
"The Influence of J. Walter Fewkes on Nampeyo:
Fact or Fancy?" in Albert H. Schroeder, ed., *The
Changing Ways of Southwestern Indians* (Glorieta,
New Mexico: Rio Grande Press, 1973.)

2. For a brief Hopi history relative to pottery and an
account of the activity of Thomas Keams, see Edwin
L. Wade and Lea S. McChesney, *Historic Hopi Ceramics* (Cambridge, Massachusetts: Peabody Museum Press. 1981) pp. 13-15.

3. Ruth L. Bunzel, *The Pueblo Potter*, Reprint:
1929 (New York: Dover Publishing Co.).

4. Prayer-feathers, prayer-plumes or bahoes are rit-
ual paraphernalia made in precise traditional ways.
For more information see index under prayer-feath-
ers in Alexander M. Stephen, edited by Elsie Clews
Parsons, *Hopi Journal*, Reprint: AMS 1969 (New
York: Columbia University Press, 1936).

Eunice (Fawn) Navasie
(b. 1924)

79.
Olla (exh. no. 11)
Hopi, Second Mesa, 1984
Earthenware; white, red and black slip
H. 6⅞ in., DIAM. (max.) 8 in.

Painted on base: FAWN (inside of symbol of a
fawn)
Gift of a Friend of the Department of American Decorative Arts and Sculpture 1984.539

Old adobe homes of the several Hopi Pueblo
villages mingle and rise out of three sandstone
mesa tops reminding one of how intimately
the Hopi live with the earth. Ever present and
breaking the horizon to the west, are the San
Francisco Peaks, a mountain range sacred to
the Hopis and home to the supernatural ancestors called Katcinas, who are Rainbringers.
The Puebloan community holds that it is the
responsibility of all members to persuade the
supernaturals to provide the necessary life-
sustaining rains and balance to the earth.

Furthest to the east is First Mesa on which
is the Pueblo of Walpi, Fawn Navasie's ancestral home. Navasie lives and works in the
Keams Canyon area between First and Second Mesa.[1] A member of the Water Clan,
Navasie speaks of feeding water to the

Katcinas from water vessels such as this during the Katcina dances. According to Navasie,
before a thunderstorm the thunderbird flies
"like crazy up and down" making the sound
of thunder. Thus the thunderbird becomes
the mythic Rainbird, who brings rain to the
parched Hopi earth. The presence of the
thunderbird on the water jar assures the Hopi
that the olla will be full of water, for when the
Hopis see the thunderbird, they know the rain
will follow.[2]
L.L.F.

1. In the summer of 1984 Jonathan Fairbanks visited with Fawn Navasie in Keams Canyon, Arizona,
and collected this olla. See data folder, American
Decorative Arts and Sculpture, Museum of Fine
Arts, Boston.

2. The iconography of this olla and the story of the
thunderbird was explained by Fawn Navasie in conversation with the author in the spring of 1990.

Lillian Salvadore
(b. 1944)

80. (color plate)
Olla (exh. no. 13)
Acoma, New Mexico, 1984
Earthenware, white, black and red slip
H. 9 in., DIAM. (max.) 11¼ in.

Painted on base: ACOMA NM/lilly, 84279
Gift of a Friend of the Department of American Decorative Arts and Sculpture. 1984.540

The work of the traditional potter Lillian Salvadore embodies the Puebloan respect for and continuity with the ways of prehistoric and ancestral cultures of the Southwest. The traditional potter does not seek to imitate the past, but rather looks to the past as a source. This pot makes clear the potter's concern with maintaining a connection with the past that is wholly within the twentieth century – traditions responsive to the changing world of the Southwest Puebloan.

Acoma pottery has consistently commanded respect for its beauty and technical excellence. The clay, which is prayerfully collected from Acoma sources, fires uncommonly hard and enables the potter to produce traditional, hand-coiled pots with remarkably thin walls. To keep the vessel from cracking during the firing process the potter must add a temper to the clay. For generations Acoma women have fired their pottery with a temper of broken, powdered sherds of ancient pottery. Acoma potters like Lillian Salvadore value the notion that their pots contain, literally, generations of pots.[1]

Pottery designs are respectfully conveyed from generation to generation. Lillian Salvadore received this, "her favorite design," from her Eagle clan grandmother, Pablito Concho (see cat. no. 14).[2] The traditional four-point design, Salvadore explains, refers to the four directions of the earth or the four seasons.[3] The body of the olla holds the

greatest proportion of images, and, mimicking the vast enveloping Southwest sky, these images represent the billowing, rain-bringing clouds. Encircling the neck, or sky, is a repeated symbol that refers to the thunderbird or eagle. Inside the neck, a band of red slip refers to the rainbow. These rain and sky symbols arise out of the relatively shallow red band at the foot of the water jar which represents the earth. Lillian Salvadore, empowered by the wisdom of the ancestors, has made the past present within this remarkable olla.
L.L.F.

1. Larry Frank and Francis H. Harlow, *Historic Pottery of the Pueblo Indians, 1600-1880* (West Chester, Pennsylvania: Schiffer Publishing Ltd., 1990), pp. 119-122.

2. Information gathered during a visit with Lillian and Wayne Salvadore by the author in July 1990.

3. Information taken from Lillian Salvadore's conversational remarks with Jonathan Fairbanks the summer of 1984, when he purchased this water jar and notes given to the Museum by Wayne Salvadore, Lillian's husband. See data folder, American Decorative Arts and Sculpture, Museum of Fine Arts, Boston.

Pablito Concho
(b. about 1900)

81.
Olla (exh. no. 14)
Acoma, New Mexico, 1985
Earthenware; white, black and red slip
H. 6 in., DIAM. (max.) 7 in.

Painted on base: Acoma/(feather symbol;
Signed in script: Pablito Concho
Gift of a Friend of the Department of American Decorative Arts and Sculpture 1985.449

The relation of Acoma potters Pablito Concho and Lillian Salvadore (see no. 13) is a traditional one that demonstrates the vigorous cultural continuity in Acoma today. The harmony of Acoma society depends largely on a strong matrilineal and extended family kinship system. As with other aspects of Acoma culture, the art of pottery-making has traditionally passed from mother to daughter as well as through a variety of kinship relations. The custom of handing down technical knowledge and design motifs makes concrete the memory of ancient ancestors. Pablito Concho values the design on this water jar because it was given to her to carry on, given long ago by her ancient ancestors and most recently by her mother from whom she learned pottery-making. Concho claims to know the truth of the long lineage of this design, for she found prehistoric pottery of the

same motif concealed in the walls of her ancestral home in Sky City.[1] The interlocking zig-zag configurations represent birds, the circles the bird's eyes.

Pablito Concho and Lillian Salvadore are members of the Eagle Clan. As a potter of more than sixty years Concho offered a role-model as well as significant support to Salvadore who, as a young child, gave evidence of her potential as a potter. In the same spirit as this design was given to her, Concho has given it to Salvadore, granddaughter by clan, to carry on.[2]
L.L.F.

1. Jonathan Fairbanks visited Pablito Concho in the summer of 1985 when he acquired this olla for the Museum. At that time Pablito Concho related the story of this design. See data folder, American Decorative Arts and Sculpture, Museum of Fine Arts, Boston.

2. Pablito Concho's clan relationship was related to the author by Lillian Salvadore in July 1990.

Bold numbers refer to illustrations

1.
Hohokam (300 B.C.-A.D. 1450)
Colonial Period, Santa Cruz Phase
Bowl (**74**)
Arizona, Gila or Salt Rivers, A.D. 700-900
Red-on-buff earthenware
H. 3¾ in., D. 10½ in.
Gift of Mr. and Mrs. Peter S. Lynch, Anne
and Joseph P. Pellegrino, Anonymous Gift,
and Frank B. Bemis Fund 1989.235

2.
Mogollon, Tularosa Phase
Zoomorphic effigy (**75**)
Tularosa black-on-white
Near Reserve, New Mexico, A.D. 1100-1225)
Gray earthenware, white and black slip
H. 10 in., W. 7½ in., D. 6¼ in.
Gift of a Friend of the Department of American Decorative Arts and Sculpture and Harriet Otis Cruft Fund 1989.316

3.
Mimbres
Bowl (**76**)
Classic, Style III, A.D. 1000-1150
Southwestern New Mexico
Earthenware; white and red to black slip
H. (uneven) 5⅛ in., D. 11¼ in.
Seth K. Sweetser Fund and Gift of Supporters of the Department of American Decorative Arts and Sculpture 1990.248

4.
Salado
Olla
Snowflake area, Arizona, A.D. 1150-1300)
Earthenware, slip
H. 9¼ in., D. 11½ in.
Gift of Mr. and Mrs. Peter S. Lynch, Anne
and Joseph P. Pellegrino, Anonymous Gift,
and Frank B. Bemis Fund 1989.234

5.
Anasazi (A.D. 800-1400)
Bowl
Four mile, Arizona, A.D. 1325-1450
Earthenware; slip
H. 3½ in., D. 8 in.
Gift of Mr. and Mrs. Peter S. Lynch, Anne
and Joseph P. Pellegrino, Anonymous Gift,
and Frank B. Bemis Fund 1989.238

6.
Acoma
Olla (**77**)
Acoma, New Mexico, about 1880
Earthenware; white, black and red slip
H. 11¾ in., DIAM. (max) 10½ in.
Gift of Anne and Joseph P. Pellegrino
1988.290

7.
Zia
Olla
Zia Pueblo, New Mexico, about 1890
Earthenware, slip
H. 9 in., D. 11 in.
Frank B. Bemis Fund 1987.421

8.
Santo Domingo
Dough bowl
Santo Domingo Pueblo, New Mexico,
1910-1920
Earthenware, slip
H. 7¾ in., D. 16½ in.
Gift of Abram T. Collier and Arthur Mason
Knapp Fund 1985.47

9.
Attributed to Old Nampeyo of Hano (about
1850-1942)
Bowl (**78**)
Hano, Arizona, about 1890
Sikyatki Revival
Earthenware; red and black slip
H. 4 in., DIAM. (max) 13 in.
Gift of Laura F. Andreson 1984.626

10.
Jar
Santa Clara Pueblo, New Mexico, about
1900
Earthenware; slip
H. 10 in., DIAM. (max) 11¾ in.
Gift of Laura F. Andreson 1984.632

11.
Eunice (Fawn) Navasie (b. 1924)
Olla (**79**)
Hopi, Second Mesa, about 1984
Earthenware; white, red, and black slip
H. 6⅞ in., DIAM. (max) 8 in.
Signed on bottom: "FAWN" within figure of
fawn
Gift of a Friend of the Department of American Decorative Arts and Sculpture 1984.539

12.
Helen Shupla (1916-1985)
Olla
Santa Clara Pueblo, New Mexico, 1984
Earthenware, slip
H. 8 in., DIAM. (rim) 3⅜ in.
Inscribed on bottom: (in script) Helen
Shupla/Santa Clara/Pueblo/10-27-84
Alice M. Bartlett Fund 1986.259

13.
Lillian Salvadore (b. 1944)
Olla (**80**)
Acoma Pueblo, New Mexico, 1984
Earthenware, white, black, and red slip
H. 9 in., DIAM. (max) 11¼ in.
Painted on base: "ACOMA NM / lilly 84279"
Gift of a Friend of the Department of American Decorative Arts and Sculpture 1984.540

14.
Pablito Concho (b. about 1900)
Olla (**81**)
Acoma, New Mexico, 1985
Earthenware; white, black, and red slip
H. 6 in., DIAM. (max) 7 in.
Signed on bottom: "Acoma / (feather symbol)
/ Pablito Concho"
Gift of a Friend of the Department of American Decorative Arts and Sculpture 1985.449

15.
Loretta Joe (b. 1960)
Olla
Acoma, New Mexico, 1982
Earthenware; slip
H. 12 in., DIAM. (max) 11 in.
Signed in slip on bottom:
"L/JOE/ACOMA/N.M."
Gift of Dr. and Mrs. R. Ted Steinbock
1986.201

16.
Seferina Ortiz (b. 1931)
Story Teller Figure
Cochiti Pueblo, New Mexico, 1985
Earthenware; slip
H. 8⅝ in., w. 8¼ in.
Signed on bottom of proper left foot: (in
script) Seferina Ortiz/Cochiti Pueblo/1985
Gift of a Friend of the Department of American Decorative Arts and Sculpture 1985.455

17.
Leather Great Chair (1)
Boston, Massachusetts, 1665-1680
Oak, maple; original upholstery foundation,
leather cover, and brass nails
H. 38 in., w. 23⅝ in., D. 16⅜ in.
Seth K. Sweetser Fund 1977.711

18.
Chest of Drawers with Doors (2)
New Haven, Connecticut, 1670-1700
Oak, walnut, cedar, pine
H. 36⅜ in., w. 44⅜ in., D. 22¾ in.
Edwin E. Jack Fund 1980.274

19.
Attributed to Benjamin Clark (1644-1724)
Board and Trestles (3)
Medfield, Massachusetts, 1690-1720
Silver maple and white pine
H. 26³⁄₁₆ in., w. 24¾ in., L. 108½ in.
Frederick Brown Fund and Helen and Alice
Colburn Fund 1980.446

20.
Attributed to the Symonds Shops
Chest with Drawer (4)
Salem, Massachusetts, 1660-1700
Oak, maple, walnut, cedar
H. 28⅞ in., w. 46 in., D. 20¾ in.
Frank Bemis Fund 1984.88

21.
Goblet
England, 1690-1700
Blown colorless lead glass
H. 10⅝ in., DIAM. (max) 6⅛ in.
Gift of the Seminarians 1981.90

22.
Richard Conyers (about 1668-1708)
Tankard (49)
Boston, Massachusetts, 1697-1708
Silver
H. 5 in., w. 5½ in., DIAM. (base) 3⅞ in.
Marked to right of handle and on top of lid:

"RC" below a crown within a shield
Gift of Stuart Alan Goldman and Marion E.
Davis Fund 1980.278

23.
Edward Winslow (1669-1753)
Candlestick (one of a pair)
Boston, Massachusetts, 1710-1720
Silver
H. 7⅝ in., w. 4⅞ in.
Marked on base: "EW" over a fleur-de-lis
within a shield
Bequest of Mr. and Mrs. Horace Havemeyer
1983.162

24.
Chest-on-Chest (5)
Boston, Massachusetts, 1715-1725
Black walnut, burl walnut veneer, eastern
white pine
H. 70¾ in., w. 42¼ in., D. 21½ in.
Gift of a Friend of the Department of American Decorative Arts and Sculpture and Otis
Norcross Fund 1986.240

25.
John Coney (1655/56-1722)
Punch Bowl (50)
Boston, Massachusetts, about 1710
Silver
H. 5 in., DIAM. (max) 9⅝ in.
Marked on bottom: crowned "IC" set over
coney within shield
Theodora Wilbour Fund in memory of Charlotte Beebe Wilbour 1972.913

26.
John Coney (1655/56-1722)
Baptismal Basin (48)
Boston, Massachusetts, about 1718
Silver
H. 3¼ in., DIAM. (max) 17 in.
Marked on bottom: crowned "IC" over coney
within shield
Gift of a Friend of the Department and Edward J. and Mary S. Holmes Fund 1984.208

John Burt (1692/93-1745/46)
Pair of Flagons
Boston, Massachusetts, about 1722
Silver
H. 14³⁄₁₆ in., w. 9½ in., DIAM. (base) 7½ in.
Marked on body to left of handle
thumbpiece: crowned "IB" above a pellet in a
shield
Gift of a Friend of the Department and Edward J. and Mary S. Holmes Fund 1984.204
and 205

27.
John Coney (1655/66-1722)
Chocolate Pot (51)
Boston, Massachusetts, 1710-1722
Silver, wood
H. 9⁷⁄₁₆ in., DIAM. (base) 4⁷⁄₁₆ in.
Marked on bezel, near lid above spout, and
on bottom: crowned "IC" over coney within a
shield

Gift of Dr. Lamar Soutter and Theodora
Wilbour Fund in Memory of Charlotte Beebe
Wilbour 1976.771

28.
Clothespress (6)
Boston, Massachusetts, 1740-1750
Mahogany, chestnut, white pine
H. 90¾ in., w. 45 in., D. 22¼ in.
Gift of the Friends of the Department of
American Decorative Arts and Sculpture
1987.254

29.
Jacob Hurd (1702/3-1758)
Teakettle-on-Stand (52)
Boston, Massachusetts, 1730-1740
Silver
H. 14⅜ in., D. 7½ in.
Marked on lid: "HURD" in ellipse; marked on
later burner: "N. HARDING & CO / BOSTON /
coin"
Gift of Esther Lowell Abbott in memory of
her mother, Esther Lowell Cunningham,
Granddaughter of Jarves Russell Lowell
1971.341

30.
Jacob Hurd (1702/3-1758)
*Small-Sword with Scabbard and Waistbelt
with Frog* (53)
Boston, Massachusetts, 1735
Silver, steel, leather
L. 30½ in.
Marked on shell of hilt: "HURD" in ellipse
Gift of Jane Bortman Larus in honor of
Kathryn C. Buhler and in recognition of her
warm friendship and association with Mark
Bortman and Jane B. Larus 1984.109

31.
Chest-on-Chest (7)
Boston, Massachusetts, about 1770
Mahogany, white pine
H. 83 in., w. 45 in., D. 21 in.
Bequest of Amelia Peabody 1984.520

32.
Desk-and-Bookcase (8)
Salem, Massachusetts, 1760-1780
Mahogany, white pine
H. 99¾ in., w. 46½ in., D. 25 in.
Gift of Lucy Davis Donovan, Emily Lincoln
Lewis and Mary Lowell Warren in Memory
of their Mother, Mary Lowell Davis
1989.308

33.
Double Chairback Settee
Boston, Massachusetts, 1770-1780
Mahogany, maple, and pine
H. 37½ in., w. 63 in., D. 21¼ in.
William Francis Warden Fund 1977.714

34.
Zachariah Brigden (1734-1787)
Teapot
Boston, Massachusetts, 1760
Silver, ivory

H. 6 in., DIAM. (base) 2¾ in.
Marked on bottom: "Z Brigden" within
cartouche
Theodora Wilbour Fund in memory of Charlotte Beebe Wilbour 1971.50

35.
Benjamin Burt (1729-1805)
Engraving by Nathaniel Hurd (1729/30-
1777)
Teapot (**54**)
Boston, Massachusetts, 1763
Silver with ebonized wooden handle
H. 5⁷⁄₁₆ in., w. 9¼ in., D. 4¼ in.
Marked on bottom: "BENJAMIN / BURT" in
cartouche
Gift of Jane Bortman Larus in memory of
Mrs. Llora Bortman 1985.16

36.
Paul Revere (1735-1818)
Tankard (**55**)
Boston, Massachusetts, 1768
Silver
H. 9¼ in., w. 7 in., D. 5 in.
Marked left of handle: "REVERE" in rectangle
Gift of Edward N. Lamson, Barbara T. Lam-
son, Edward F. Lamson, Howard J. Lamson
and Susan L. Strickler 1986.678

37.
John Cogswell (1738-1818)
Chest-on-Chest (**9**)
Boston, Massachusetts, 1782
Mahogany, white pine
H. 89½ in., w. 43½ in., D. 23½ in.
Signed on inside surface of back board of
lower case: "J. Cogswel"; signed on top of
lower case: "Made by John / Cogswell in
midle street / Boston 1782"
William Francis Warden Fund 1973.289

38.
High Chest of Drawers (**10**)
Newtown, Connecticut, 1760-1780
Cherry, yellow poplar, oak
H. 82 in., w. 42½ in., D. 20¾ in.
Gift of a Friend of the Department of Ameri-
can Decorative Arts and Sculpture, Eddy
Nicholson, The Arthur Tracy Cabot Fund
and Anonymous Gift 1988.16

39.
Elias Pelletreau (1726-1810)
Tankard
Southhampton, New York, about 1760
Silver
H. 7⅞ in., w. 7¾ in.
Marked on each side of handle: "EP" in
rectangle
Bequest of Katharine Lane Weems 1989.515

40.
Joseph Richardson (1711-1784)
Sauceboat (one of a pair)
Philadelphia, Pennsylvania, about 1750
Silver

H. 4 in., L. 7¾ in.
Marked: "IR" with leaf device above within
rectangle
Gift of a Friend of the Department of American Decorative Arts and Sculpture 1985.412-
413

41.
American China Manufactory (1770-1772)
Fruit Basket (**37**)
Philadelphia, Pennsylvania, 1771-1772
Soft-paste porcelain, underglaze blue
decoration
H. 2¹¹⁄₁₆ in., DIAM. 6⅞ in.
Marked on bottom: "Z"
Frederick Brown Fund 1977.621

42.
New Bremen Glass Manufactory (1784-1795)
Case Bottle
Established by John Frederick Amelung
(1741-1798)
Frederick County, Maryland, 1788
Blown and engraved glass
H. 7¼ in., w. 3¼ in., D. 3¼ in.
H.E. Bolles Fund 1973.552

43.
Work Table (**11**)
Boston, Massachusetts, 1795-1805
Mahogany, thuya burl veneer, birch veneer,
rosewood and holly inlay; new bag
H. 28 in., w. 19⅝ in., D. 15⅜ in.
Bequest of Priscilla G. Hall 1990.172

44.
Pier Table (one of a pair) (**12**)
Boston or Salem, Massachusetts, 1800-1810
Mahogany, mahogany veneer, burl, rosewood
veneer, birch, white pine, yellow poplar and
brass.
H. 35 in., w. 55½ in., D. 24 in.
Gift of Richard Edwards 1972.429

45.
Adam Hains (1768-after 1820)
Upholstery attributed to George Bertault
(working 1793)
Armchair (one of a pair) (**13**)
Philadelphia, Pennsylvania, about 1792-1797
Mahogany; original upholstery foundation
with modern cover fabric
H. 33 in., w. 23 in., D. 19 in.
Paper label inside rear seat rail: "ALL / KINDS
OF / CABINET AND CHAIRWORK / DONE BY /
ADAM HAINS / NO. 135. NORTH THIRD-STREET
/ PHILADELPHIA"
Otis Norcross Fund, William Francis Warden
Fund, Gift of a Friend of the Department
1979.486

46.
Mourning Pendant (**56**)
Boston, Massachusetts, 1787
Gold frame with glass cover; ivory with water
color and gold thread; plaited hair on reverse
H. 1⅞ in., w. 1⅛ in.
Gift of Mr. Charles H. Wood 1985.1025

Mourning Pin
Boston, Massachusetts, 1787
Gold frame with glass cover, plaited hair
H. 1⅞ in., w. 1⅛ in.
Gift of Mr. Charles H. Wood 1985.1027

47.
Charles Boehme (1774-1868)
Tea Service
Baltimore, Maryland, 1800-1805
Silver, ivory
Teapot: H. 6¾ in., w. 10¼ in.; marked on
bottom: "C L Boehme" in rectangle and eagle
hallmark. Slop bowl: H. 4⅞ in., DIAM. 6⁵⁄₁₆
in.; marked on inside and outside edges of
base plinth: "C L Boehme" in rectangle and
eagle hallmark. Sugar bowl: H. 10¾ in.,
DIAM. 4⅝ in.; marked on outside edge of base
plinth: "C L Boehme" in rectangle and eagle
hallmark. Creampot: H. 7¹¹⁄₁₆ in., L. 5½ in.;
marked on underside base: "C L Boehme" in
oval
Gift of Miss Martha May Eliot, M. D., and
Miss Abigail Adams Eliot 1971.309-312

48.
Attributed to Charles-Honore Lannuier
(1779-1819)
Pier Table
New York, New York, about 1815
Mahogany, white pine, yellow polar; mahog-
any and rosewood veneers; giling, antique
vert; brass stringing and marble
H. 33⅜ in., w. 41¾ in., D. 18¹³⁄₁₆ in.
Gift of W.N. Banks Foundation 1975.274

49.
Side Chair (**14**)
Baltimore, Maryland, 1815-1825
Wood, cane, painted decoration
H. 31⅞ in., w. 20⅛ in., D. 21 in.
Gift of Jean and Michael Dingman and Otis
Norcross Fund 1981.26

50.
Thomas Warner (1780-1828) and Andrew El-
licot Warner (1786-1870)
Commemorative Sword and Scabbard
Baltimore, Maryland, 1805-1812
Silver, ivory, steel
L. 39 in.
Marked on underside of the crossguard: "T &
A.E.WARNER" within rectangle and eagle's
head hallmark
Gift of William N. Banks Foundation
1973.481

51.
Higbie and Crosby (active 1825-1830)
Tea Service (**57**)
New York, New York, 1825-30
Silver
Teapot: H. 10¼ in., w. 12 in., DIAM. (base) 5
in.; marked: "HIGBIE & CROSBY / (face in pro-
file) (crowned head) C (star)." Covered sugar
bowl: H. 9¾ in., w. 9½ in., DIAM. (base) 4¾
in.; marked: "(face in profile) (crowned head)

C (star) / HIGBIE & CROSBY." Creamer: H. 8 in., W. 7 in., DIAM. (base) 3¾ in. Marked: "(face in profile) (crowned head) C (star)."
Gift of Dr. and Mrs. Roger G. Gerry 1975.649-651

52.
Center Table
Boston or Salem, Massachusetts, 1825-1835
White pine, rosewood veneer; gilt and marble
H. 30½ in., DIAM. 40¾ in.
Gift of the Seminarians, William J. Banks, Jr. and Frank B. Bemis Fund 1984.162

53.
Attributed to John Finlay (1771-1851) or Hugh Finlay (1781-1831)
Grecian Couch (15)
Baltimore, Maryland, 1820-1840
Yellow poplar, cherry, white pine; rosewood graining and gilded painting; partial original upholstery foundation and new foundation materials, cover, and trim
H. 35¾ in., W. 91½ in., D. 24¼ in.
Gift of Mr. and Mrs. Amos B. Hostetter, Jr., Anne and Joseph P. Pellegrino, Mr. and Mrs. Peter S. Lynch, Mr. William N. Banks, Jr., Eddy G. Nicholson, Mr. and Mrs. John Lastavica, Mr. and Mrs. Daniel F. Morley, and Mary S. and Edward J. Holmes Fund 1988.530

54.
Celery Vase
American, 1800-1825
Engraved flint glass
H. 5 in., DIAM. 4 in.
Dorothy-Lee Jones Fund 1975.20

55.
Kensington Glass Works (1818- about 1838)
Portrait Flask: Benjamin Franklin and T.W. Dyott, M.D.
Kensington, Philadelphia, Pennsylvania, 1826-28
Blown-molded pale green glass
H. 8 in., W. 5⅛ in., D. 3 in.
Gift of the Estate of Philip B. Holmes in honor of George C. Seybolt 1987.731

56.
South Boston Flint Glass Works (1812-1827) or Phoenix Glass Works (1819/20-1870)
Decanter (68)
Attributed to Thomas Cains (1779-1865)
South Boston, Massachusetts, 1813-1835
Free-blown colorless flint glass
H. 10½ in., DIAM. 5¼ in.
The William H. Fenn III Glass Collection 1978.698

57.
Boston and Sandwich Glass (1828-1850)
Covered Sugar Bowl
Sandwich, Massachusetts, 1826-1840
Molded-blown colorless glass
H. 6 in., D. 4⅜ in.

John Wheelock and John Morse Elliot Fund 1981.48

58.
Liberty
Possibly Massachusetts, 1790-1800
White pine, paint
H. 58 in., W. 24½ in.
H.E. Bolles Fund 1979.163

59.
Horatio Greenough (1805-1852)
Arno (30)
Florence, Italy, 1838
Marble
H. 25¼ in., D. 22½ in., L. 51½ in.
Arthur Tracy Cabot Fund 1973.601

60.
Center Table (16)
Possibly New York, New York, about 1850
Rosewood and rosewood veneer; new marble top
H. 30 in., DIAM. 37 in.
Edwin E. Jack Fund 1981.402

61.
Boston and Sandwich Glass Company (1828-1850)
Dish with Cover and Tray
Sandwich, Massachusetts, 1835-1850
Colorless pressed glass
H. 5 in, W. 6¾ in., D. 5 in.
Given by Kenneth and Mary Jane Wakefield in memory of Ruth Wakefield 1979.693

62.
Ignatius Lutz (active 1844-1860)
Sideboard (17)
Philadelphia, Pennsylvania, 1850-1860
Oak, yellow poplar; marble
H. 94 in., W. 74 in., D. 25 in.
Stenciled label on back of lower section: "FROM / I. LUTZ' / CABINET WAREHOUSE / No. 121 S. 11th St. / PHIL"
Gift of the Estate of Richard Bruce E. Lacont 1990.1

63.
Shreve, Stanwood & Co. (1860-1869)
Coffee and Tea Service
Boston, Massachusetts, 1867
Silver
Coffee pot: H. 10¼ in., W. 10¼ in., D. 4¾ in.; marked on bottom: "Shreve, Stanwood & Co. / Boston (in rectangle) / Sterling" Teapot: H. 8¾ in., W. 10 in., D. 4⅝ in.; marked on bottom: "Shreve, Stanwood & Co. / Boston (in rectangle) / Sterling" Teapot: H. 8¾in., W. 10¼ in., D. 4⅝ in.; marked on bottom: "Shreve, Stanwood & Co. / Boston (rectangle) / Sterling" Waste bowl: H. 4¼ in., W. 6½ in., D. 4½ in.; marked on bottom: "Shreve, Stanwood & Co. / Boston (in rectangle) / Sterling" Sugar bowl: H. 7½ in., W. 8¼ in., D. 4¼ in.; marked on bottom: "Shreve, Stanwood & Co. / Boston (in rectangle) / Sterling"

Creampot: H. 6¼ in., W. 6⅝ in., D. 3½ in.; no mark visible as lead fills the cavity of the foot. Creampot: H. 5⅛ in., W. 6¾ in., D. 4¼ in.; marked on bottom:""Shreve, Stanwood & Co. / Boston (in rectangle) / Sterling"
Gift of Priscilla L. Waite 1984.569-575

64.
Nelson Gustafsson (active 1860s-1880s)
Cabinet
New York, New York, 1860-1880
Mahogany, rosewood, exotic wood marquetry; porcelain; brass
H. 60⅝ in., W. 74½ in., D. 16½ in.
Stamped on top of ebonized pilasters, on bottom rail of central door, on bottom rail of left and right front panels; on back stretcher of base, and on back board: "N. GUSTAFSSON"
Edwin E. Jack Fund 1981.400

65.
Herter Brothers (1865-1905)
Side Chair (18)
New York, New York, about 1880
Cherry, lightwood marquetry; ebonized finish and gilded detailing; original upholstery foundation with new cover fabric and trim
H. 34¼ in., W. 17 in., D. 18¼ in.
Gift of the Estate of Richard Bruce E. Lacont 1990.105

66.
Tiffany & Co. (1850-)
Coffee Pot
New York, New York, 1856-1859)
Silver
H. 10¾ in., W. 7¾ in.
Marked on bottom: "TIFFANY & CO. / 774 / M / ENGLISH SILVER / 925-1000 / M / 5245 / 550 BROADWAY"
Marion Davis Fund 1981.403

67.
New England Glass Company (1818-1888)
Covered Jar
Engraved by Louis Friedrich Vaupel (1824-1903)
East Cambridge, Massachusetts, about 1875
Colorless lead glass
H. 4⅝ in., W. 3 in. D. 3 in.
Gift of Mrs. Mildred M. March 1976.633

68.
Low Art Tile Works (1878-1907)
Tile
Chelsea, Massachusetts, 1881-1895
White earthenware with glossy glaze
H. 6 1/16 in., W. 6 1/16 in.
Marked on back: "J. & J.G. LOW. / PATENT / ART TILE WORKS / CHELSEA / MASS. U.S.A. / COPYRIGHT 1881 BY J. & J.G. LOW"
Gift of Prof. Emeritus F.H.Norton and the Department of Metallurgy and Materials Science at the Massachusetts Institute of Technology
71.545

69.
S. Karpen & Bros. (1883-1952)
Armchair (**19**)
Chicago, Illinois, 1901-1910
Mahogany, maple; gold leaf; original foundation and final cover with some new final cover on the seat, back, and arms
H. 42 in., w. 32½ in., D. 25½ in.
Gift of Daniel and Jessie Lie Farber 1986.749

70.
Gorham Manufacturing Company (1831-)
Punch Bowl and Ladle (**58**)
Providence, Rhode Island, 1885
Silver
Bowl: H. 10⅛ in., D. 15¾ in.; marked on bottom: "(lion) (anchor) G / (wolf's head) / 1980 / STERLING" Ladle: L. 14 in.; marked: "STERLING"
Edwin E. Jack Fund 1980.383, 384

71.
Gorham Manufacturing Company (1831-)
Pitcher (**59**)
Providence, Rhode Island, about 1885
Silver
H. 10 in., w. 7¼ in., D. 4½ in.
Marked on bottom: "(lion) G (anchor) / STERLING / 1295 / (wolf's head)"
Edwin E. Jack Fund 1983.331

72.
Rookwood Pottery Company (1880-1960)
Gorham Manufacturing Company (1831-)
Pitcher (**38**)
Decorated by Constance Amelia Baker (active 1892-1904)
Cincinnati, Ohio, 1894
White earthenware, decorated with brown, yellow, green, and blue slip and covered with transparent glossy glaze; silver deposit decoration.
H. 6⅝ in., w. 8¼ in., D. 6 in.
Marked on bottom: "(seven flames) / R(reversed)P / 52/ D / w." Signed on bottom: "CAB." Marked on silver: "R1056 GORHAM MFG CO."
Edwin E. Jack Fund 1989.200

73.
John La Farge (1835-1910)
Morning Glories (**71**)
Six-paneled window from William Watts Sherman House, Newport, Rhode Island
Boston, Massachusetts, 1877-78
Leaded stained glass
H. 86½ in., w. 72 in.
Gift of James F. and Jean Baer O'Gorman 1974.498

74.
Buffet (**20**)
Vincennes, Indiana, about 1800
Yellow poplar, curly maple
H. 46¼ in., w. 48 in., D. 24¼ in.
Gift of Daniel and Jessie Lie Farber and Frank Bemis Fund 1989.50

75.
Heinrich Kuenemann II (1843-1914)
Wardrobe (**21**)
Fredericksburg, Texas, about 1870
Pine
H. 87¼ in., w. 56½ in., D. 23½ in.
Gift of Mrs. Charles L. Bybee 1990.483

76.
Pitcher
Pennsylvania, 1790-1830
Earthenware with lead glaze
H. 7⅝ in., D. 4¾ in.
Hezekiah E. Bolles Fund 1971.386

77.
Platter
Probably Pennsylvania, 1800-1900
Earthenware with slip decoration and lead glaze
H. 2½ in., w. 13¼ in., D. 10½ in.
Gift of C. Malcolm and Joan P. Watkins in Memory of Lura Woodside Watkins 1987.688

78.
Thomas Crawford (1813-1857)
Orpheus and Cerberus (**31**)
Rome, Italy, 1839 (modeled), 1843 (carved)
Marble
H. 67½ in., w. 36 in., D. 54 in.
Inscribed on base, left: "T. G. CRAWFORD, FECIT. / ROMAE / MDCCCXLIII
Gift of Mr. and Mrs. Cornelius Vermeule III 1975.800

79.
William Wetmore Story (1819-1895)
Sappho (**32**)
Rome, Italy, 1863
Marble
H. 54⅞ in., w. 32⅛ in., D. 34 in.
Signed on back: "WWS / ROMA 1863"
Otis Norcross Fund 1977.772

80.
Augustus Saint-Gaudens (1848-1907)
Head of Victory (**33**)
Paris or New York, 1907
Bronze, marble
H. 8 in., w. 7 in., D. 6¼ in.
Signed on proper left side of neck: "A . SAINT . GAVDENS . M · C · MV ."
Helen and Alice Colburn Fund 1977.600

81.
Charles Rohlfs Workshop (1898-1928)
Bench
Designed by Charles Rohlfs (1853-1936)
Buffalo, New York, about 1900
Oak, iron, copper
H. 45½ in., w. 35⅛ in., D. 21½ in.
Branded on proper left inside of chest: "R" within bow saw
Gift of a Friend of the Department of American Decorative Arts and the Arthur Mason Knapp Fund 1983.14

82.
Arthur J. Stone (1847-1938)
Jardiniere (**60**)
Gardner, Massachusetts, about 1902
Copper with silver details
H. 5 in., DIAM. (rim) 7½ in.
Marked on bottom: "Stone" with hammer crossing the t
Gift of Alma Bent 1987.464

83.
Robert Jarvie (1865-1941)
Hot Beverage Service
Chicago, Illinois, about 1915
Silver; wood
Tray: H. 1 in., w. 21 in., D. 15¾ in.; marked on bottom: "STERLING Jarvie 2015/1" Coffee pot: H. 7¾ in., w. 7½ in., D. 3¼ in.; marked on bottom: "STERLING Jarvie 2010/1" Hot water pot: H. 8¾ in., w. 9 in., D. 3¾ in.; marked: "STERLING Jarvie 2011/1" Tea pot: H. 6 in., w. 10 in., D. 4½ in.; marked on bottom: "STERLINGJarvie 2012/1" Sugar bowl: H. 3½ in., w. 4½ in., D. 3½ in.; marked on bottom: "STERLING Jarvie 2014/1" Creamer: H. 5 in., w. 6 in., D. 2¾ in.; marked on bottom: "STERLING Jarvie 2013/1"
Gift of a Friend of the Department of American Decorative Arts and Sculpture, John H. and Ernestine A. Payne Fund, and Curator's Fund 1987.556-561

84.
George C. Gebelein (1878-1945)
Coffee and Tea Service (**61**)
Boston, Massachusetts, 1929
Silver, ebony
Tea kettle on stand: H. 12¼ in., w. 9 in.; marked on base: "GEBELEIN (in rectangle) / STERLING / BOSTON." COFFEE POT: H. 8¾ in., w. 9½in.; marked on base: "Gebelein (in keyhole cartouche) / STERLING / Boston." Teapot: H. 8¾ in., w. 9½ in.; marked on base: "Gebelein (in keyhole cartouche) / STERLING / Boston." Creamer: H. 6¼ in., w. 4⅝ in.; marked on base: "Gebelein" (in keyhole cartouche), "STERLING", and "Boston." Covered sugar bowl: H. 8½ in., w. 3¾ in.; marked on base: "Gebelein" (in keyhole cartouche), "STERLING", and "Boston."
Anonymous Gift 1986.778-782

85.
Josephine Hartwell Shaw (active about 1900-1935)
Necklace (**62**)
Boston, about 1915
Gold, glass, jade
L. 20 in.
Marked on applied tab: "J. H. Shaw"
Gift of Mrs. Atherton Loring 1984.947

86.
Edward Everett Oakes (1891-1960)
Brooch
Boston, about 1925

Gold, pearls, beryl
H. ⅞ in., W. 1¼ in.
Gift of Daniel and Jessie Lie Farber 1986.764

87.
Newcomb Pottery (1895-1940)
Vase (39)
Thrown by Joseph Fortune Meyer (1848-1931)
Decorated by Marie (d. 1954) and Emilie de Hoa LeBlanc (d. 1941)
New Orleans, Louisiana, 1902
Buff colored earthenware with blue-green glossy glaze
H. 11⅜ in., DIAM. (rim) 3⅝ in.
Marks: incised on bottom: "JM" in conjoined cipher, "EL EB" in conjoined cipher; blue underglaze mark on bottom: "NC" cipher, "M-LEB" cipher, and "W44" cipher
Laurie Crichton Memorial Fund 1980.226

88.
Grueby-Faience Company (1894-1909) or Grueby Faience and Tile Company (1909-1920)
Tile (40)
Designed by Addison B. Le Boutillier (1872-1951)
Boston, Massachusetts, 1906-20
Light buff earthenware with matte glaze
H. 8 1/16 in., W. 8 1/16 in., D. 1 in.
Marked on back: "GRUEBY / BOSTON"
Gift of C. Malcolm and Joan P. Watkins in Memory of Lura Woodside Watkins 1987.662

89.
Marblehead Pottery (1904-1936)
Bowl (41)
Marblehead, Massachusetts, about 1910-1915
Earthenware with incised and glazed decoration
H. 3⅞ in., DIAM. 10½ in.
Stamped twice on bottom: "M (square-rigged ship) P" within circle
Gift of John P. Axelrod 1990.48

90.
Charles Eames (1907-1978)
Side Chair, Model DCW (22)
Venice, California, 1946
Walnut plywood, rubber, metal
H. 28¾ in., W. 19¾ in., D. 20½ in.
Labeled: "Herman Miller (logo) / EVANS (logo) / Charles Eames"
Gift of Edward J. Wormley 1975.31

91.
Margret Craver (b. 1907)
Teapot (63)
Wichita, Kansas, about 1936
Silver and Gabon ebony
H. 5½ in., W. 9½ in., D. 5 in.
Marked on bottom: "C" within stylized flower

Gift in Memory of Joyce Goldberg with funds provided by Mr. John P. Axelrod, Mr. and Mrs. Sidney Stoneman, Mr. Charles Devens, Mr. and Mrs. Peter Lynch, The Seminarians, Mr. James G. Hinkle, Jr., The MFA Council and Friends 1988.533

92.
Maria Regnier (b. 1901)
Tea Service (64)
Saint Louis, Missouri, 1939
Silver, ivory
Teapot: H. 6 in., W. 11¾ in., D. 6 in.; marked "MR / STERLING / HAND WROUGHT."
Creamer: H. 2¼ in., W. 6¾ in., D. 3⅝ in.; marked: "MR / STERLING / HAND WROUGHT."
Covered sugar bowl: H. 2¾ in., W. 4½ in., D. 3½ in.; marked: "MR / STERLING / HAND WROUGHT"
Gift of John E. Goodman 1989.60-62

93.
Cowan Pottery Studio (1912-1931)
Punch bowl from the "Jazz Bowl" series (42)
Thrown by Reginald Guy Cowan
Designed and decorated by Viktor Schreckengost (b. 1906)
Rocky River, Ohio, 1931
Glazed porcelain with sgraffito decoration
H. 9 in., DIAM. (rim) 16⅞ in.
Gift of John P. Axelrod 1990.507

94.
Maija Grotell (1899-1973)
Vase
Bloomfield Hills, Michigan, 1938-1945
Glazed earthenware
H. 12¾ in., DIAM. 7¼ in.
Signed on bottom: "mg"
Axelrod Collection 1985.812

95.
Steuben Division of Corning Glass (1918-present)
Intarsia Vase (70)
Frederick Carder (1863-1963)
Corning, New York, 1920-about 1930
Blown triple-layered colorless and black glass
H. 8¾ in., DIAM. 3½ in.
Facsimile inscription engraved on lower lobe of vessel in script: "Fred'k Carder"
Gift of Prof. Emeritus F. H. Norton and the Department of Metallurgy and Materials Science at the Massachusetts Institute of Technology 1971.592

96.
Herbert Adams (1858-1945)
The Debutante (34)
New York, New York, 1914
Bronze; original wood base
H. 14½ in., W. 4½ in., D. 4½ in.
Signed: "HA MCMXIV"
Marked: "ROMAN BRONZE WORKS NY"
Gift of Jean S. and Frederic A. Sharf 1988.486

97.
Katharine Lane Weems (1899-1989)
Revolt (35)
Boston, Massachusetts, 1980 (modeled in 1926)
Bronze
H. 30½ in., L. 19¼ in., D. 6 in.
Signed at front of base: "19c80 K. LANE WEEMS"; marked at front of base: "TX"
Gift of Katharine Lane Weems 1981.664

98.
Walker Hancock (b. 1901)
Head of an Angel (36)
Lanesville, Massachusetts, 1950
Plaster
H. 32½ in., W. 21 in., D. 27 in.
Signed on proper left bottom: "Walker Hancock 1950"
Gift of Walker Hancock 1980.426

99.
George Nakashima (1905-1990)
Settee
New Hope, Pennsylvania, 1979
Walnut, ash
H. 31¼ in., W. 84¾ in., D. 34¾ in.
Purchased through Funds provided by the National Endowment for the Arts and Deborah M. Noonan Foundation 1979.275

100.
Sam Maloof (b. 1916)
Rocking Chair (23)
Alta Loma, California, 1975
Walnut, ebony
H. 45 in., W. 27¾ in., D. 46 in.
Signed on underside of seat: "MOFA BOSTON / Sam Maloof 1975 F.A.C.C. / NO 79"
Purchased through Funds Provided by the National Endowment for the Arts and The Gillette Corporation 1976.122

101.
James Prestini (b. 1908)
Bowl (24)
Chicago, Illinois, 1922-1953
Birch
H. 4⅝ in., D. 10½ in.
Marked on bottom: "PRESTINI"
Gift of James Prestini 1980.394

102.
Bob Stocksdale (b. 1913)
Bowl (25)
Berkeley, California, 1980
Macadamia wood
H. 3⅜ in., DIAM. (rim) 3¾ in.
Signed on bottom: "Macadamia / from / California / Bob Stocksdale / 1980"
Harriet Otis Cruft Fund 1980.389

103.
Edwin Scheier (b. 1910) and Mary Goldsmith (b. 1908)
Footed Bowl
Dunham, New Hampshire, about 1955
Glazed stoneware; Albany slip

H. 8¾ in., DIAM. 7⅜ in.
Marked on bottom: "Scheier
Gift of Margret Craver Withers 1990.231

104.
Otto Natzler (b. 1908) and Gertrud Amon
Natzler (1908-1971)
Bowl (**43**)
Los Angeles, California, 1957
Red earthenware with gray-earth crater glaze
H. 4⅞ in.; DIAM. (rim) 8⅞ in.
Signed: "NATZLER"; labeled: "H 451"
Anonymous Gift 1989.184

105.
Laura Andreson (b. 1902)
Bottle (**44**)
Los Angeles, California, 1983
Porcelain with white crystalline glaze
H. 8⅞ in., w. 4½ in.
Scratched on base: "Laura Andreson," "83"
in circle
Gift of Mary-Louise Meyer in memory of
Norman Meyer 1984.75

106.
Robert Turner (1913-present)
Ashanti
Alfred, New York, 1983
Stoneware
H. 12½ in., D. 10¼ in.
Marked on bottom: "TURNER"
Gift of Mary-Louise Meyer in memory of
Norman Meyer 1984.558

107.
Brother Thomas (Thomas Bezanson) (b.
1929)
Vase (**45**)
Weston Priory, Weston, Vermont, 1980
Porcelain
H. 14 in., DIAM. (max) 13 in.
Marked on bottom: "£", "2/2," "802"
Gift of Edith W. and Frederick Bloom
1981.38

108.
Harrison McIntosh (b. 1914)
Lidded Jar
Claremont, California, 1987
Porcelain with matte glaze
H. 9½ in., DIAM. (max) 6 in.
Marked on bottom: "HM" in rectangle;
sticker on bottom: "HANDTHROWN / STONE-
WARE / HARRISON / MCINTOSH / CLAREMONT /
CALIFORNIA"
Gift of Nathaniel T. Dexter 1988.302

109.
Peter Voulkos (b. 1924)
Untitled (**46**)
Berkeley, California, about 1959-1960
Glazed stoneware with epoxy paint
H. 27½ in., w. 12½ in., D. 6¼ in.
Signed in black slip near base: "Voulkos"
Anonymous Gift 1979.502

110.
Rude Osolnik (b.1915)
Vessel (**26**)
Berea, Kentucky, 1987
Birch plywood
H. 10¾ in., DIAM. (max) 9⅜ in.
Signed on base: "Osolnik Originals / Lami-
nated birch plywood / '87"
Gift of Daniel and Jessie Lie Farber 1988.234

111.
Edward Zucca (b. 1946)
XVIIIth Dynasty Television (**27**)
Woodstock, Connecticut, 1989
Honduran mahogany, yellow poplar, ebony;
gold leaf, silver leaf, rush; latex paint,
ebonizing
H. 61 in., w. 33½ in., D. 42 in.
Signed on underside of cornice at back:
"Edward / Zucca / 1989"
Gift of Anne and Ronald Abramson
1989.263

112.
Rosanne Somerson (b.1954)
Bench (**28**)
Westport, Massachusetts, 1986
Pearwood, soft curly maple, leather
H. 22¾ in., w. 57½ in., D. 22¼ in.
Signed on underside of front rail: "Assisted
by D.E. K. 8 RS (intertwined with the S sur-
mounting the R) 6 FOR MFA Thanks to R. A.
+ A. A."
Gift of Anne and Ronald Abramson 1987.40

113.
Tom Loeser (b. 1956)
Chest
Cambridge, Massachusetts, 1988
Cherry, curly maple, birch plywood; milk
paint
H. 20⅛ in., w. 59 in., D. 16 in.
Gift of the Seminarians and Anonymous Gift
1988.332

114.
Mike Shuler (b. 1950)
Bowl #422
Santa Cruz, California, 1989
Macassar ebony, Brazilian tulipwood
H. 5 in., DIAM. (lip) 12⅛ in.
Signed on bottom: "M. SHULER # 422 1989"
This project was supported in part by a grant
from the National Endowment for the Arts, a
federal agency and Supporters of The Depart-
ment of American Decorative Arts and Sculp-
ture 1990.272

115.
Mark Lindquist (b. 1949)
Ascending Bowl #12 (**29**)
Quincy, Florida, 1988
American black walnut
H. 14¼ in., DIAM. (rim) 17¾ in.
Signed on base: "Mark Lindquist / 1988 / As-
cending Bowl / #12 / Walnut
Gift of Mr. and Mrs. Sidney Stoneman
1989.205

116.
Wayne Higby (b. 1943)
Mirage Lake (**47**)
Alfred, New York, 1984
Raku-fired earthenware
H. 11⅛ in., DIAM. (rim) 18½ in.
Stamped: 84
Gift of Mary-Louise Meyer in memory of
Norman Meyer 1984.770

117.
Kreg Kallenberger (b.1950)
View from Saddleback Ridge from the Osage
Series (**72**)
Tulsa, Oklahoma, 1990
Cast optical crystal; cut, polished, sand-
blasted, and oil stained
H. 7⅜ in., w. 19½ in., D. 5½ in.
Signed on bottom proper right: "KK"
This project was supported in part by a grant
from the National Endowment for the Arts, a
Federal agency, and The Seminarians 1990.122

118.
Dan Dailey (b. 1947)
"Dense Growth" Vase from Science Fiction
Series (**73**)
Blown in Williamstown, West Virginia, and
decorated in Amesbury, Massachusetts,
1984-86
Glass and fired glass enamels
H. 11½ in., DIAM. 10 in.
Signed on vessel side just above base: "Dai-
ley;" signed on bottom: "SF-4-84 / DENSE
GROWTH"
Gift of Mr. and Mrs. John S. Clarkeson
1987.571

119.
Dale Chihuly (b. 1941)
Seven Forms (selection of)
Pilchuck, Washington, 1982
Blown glass
Gift of Michael J. Bove III 1983.518-524

120.
Albert Paley (b. 1944)
Plant Stand (**65**)
Rochester, New York, 1988-89
Mild steel; brass; slate
H. 56½ in., w. (max) 25½ in.
Marked on base: "c PALEY STUDIOS LTD.
1988"
Purchased through funds provided by The
National Endowment for the Arts and The
Seminarians 1989.78

121.
Richard Mawdsley (b. 1945)
Standing Cup (**66**)
Carterville, Illinois, 1986
Silver
H. 17⅜ in., DIAM. (max) 4¼ in.
Marked on base: "RM STERLING SN / AG"
Anonymous Gift 1988.535

122.
Charles Crowley (b. 1958)
Tea Service on Stand (67)
Waltham, Massachusetts, 1987
Silver, cast aluminum; enamel paint
H. 30 in., L. 19 in., W. 16 in.
Signed on the bottom of all three vessels:
"Charlie Crowley / 1987"
Gift of Anne and Ronald Abramson
1987.232

123.
Robert Butler (b. 1955)
Animal Bowl
Northeast, New York, 1990
Silver
H. 8½ in. W. 12½ in. D. 8 in.
Marked on base: "R BUTLER / (thistle) / 90"
Anonymous Gift 1990

124.
An Unknown Gentleman (probably John Wensley)
Boston, 1670-1680)
Oil on canvas
H. 43¾ in., W. 40 in.
Charles H. Bayley Picture and Painting Fund
1984.578

125.
Winthrop Chandler (1747-1790)
The Battle of Bunker Hill
Woodstock, Connecticut, 1780-1790
Oil on panel
H. 42 in., W. 60½ in.
Gift of Mr. and Mrs. Gardner Richardson
1982.281

126.
Gilbert Stuart (1755-1828)
Joseph Warren Revere
Boston, Massachusetts,
Oil on panel
H. 37½ in., W. 32 in.
Gift of a Friend of the Department of American Decorative Arts and Sculpture 1987.55

STAFF, VISITING COMMITTEE, VOLUNTEERS AND INTERNS

Staff

Jonathan Fairbanks (*Katharine Lane Weems Curator of American Decorative Arts and Sculpture 1971-present*)

Ellen Abernathy (*secretary 1978-1979*)

Lu Bartlett (*office assistant 1972-1973*)

Michael Brown (*curatorial assistant 1978-1980*)

Mrs. Kathryn C. Buhler (*research fellow 1972-1986**)

Rachel Camber (*department assistant 1986-1987, secretary 1984-1985*)

Diane Carlberg (*National Endowment for the Arts intern 1990*)

Beth Carver (*secretary 1974-1975*)

Vincent Cerbone (*furniture restorer 1971-1976**)

Brian Considine (*Vincent Cerbone Fellow in furniture conservation 1981-1983*)

Edward S. Cooke, Jr. (*associate curator 1990-present, assistant curator 1985-1990*)

Wendy A. Cooper (*assistant curator 1976-1977 1981-1983, special assistant 1974-1975*)

Laurie Crichton (*secretary 1976-1977**)

Lauretta Dimmick (*assistant curator 1987-1990*)

Jennifer C. Dragone (*National Museum Act intern 1987*)

Eleuthera D. du Pont (*office assistant 1974-1975*)

Robert Emlen (*Special projects assistant 1978*)

Jeannine Falino (*assistant curator 1990-present, curatorial assistant 1987-1990*)

Daniel Farber (*photographic associate 1977-1982*)

Anne Farnam (*department assistant 1974-1975*)

Linda Foss (*secretary 1989-present, typist 1988*)

Alec Graham (*Mellon fellow in furniture conservation 1980*)

Kathryn Greenthal (*consultant 1980-1986*)

Karen Guffey (*National Museum Act intern 1981*)

Deborah Hale (*secretary 1980*)

Barbara Jobe (*cataloguer 1974-1975*)

Wendy Kaplan (*research associate 1983-1987, research assistant 1980-1982*)

Karol Kaiser (*office assistant 1978*)

Paula M. Kozol (*curatorial assistant 1984-1987, National Museum Act intern 1983*)

Nina Fletcher Little (*honorary research fellow 1977-present*)

Rachel J. Monfredo (*research assistant 1990-present*)

Margaret Moody (*research assistant 1979*)

Sarah Olson (*National Museum Act intern 1978*)

Andrew Passeri (*upholstery consultant 1978-present*)

Maria Pulsone (*department assistant 1987-present*)

Mary Quinn (*department assistant 1983-1984, secretary 1981-1982**)

Jan Seidler Ramirez (*research associate 1980-1982, assistant curator 1978-1979, National Endowment for the Arts intern 1976-1977*)

Naomi Remes (*exhibition assistant 1981-1982*)

Robert Blair St. George (*research assistant 1978-1979*)

Deborah Shinn (*office assistant 1977*)

Joy Cattanach Smith (*consultant 1984-1986, curatorial assistant 1981-1984, research assistant 1980; office assistant 1979*)

Letitia Stevens (*Getty advanced intern in furniture conservation 1990-present*)

Elizabeth Sussman (*special assistant 1974-1975*)

Robert Trent (*research associate 1978-1982*)

Robert Walker (*furniture conservator 1984-present, furniture restorer 1977-1983, associate furniture restorer, 1974-1976*)

Susan Odell Walker (*conservation assistant 1989-present, conservation technician 1987-1989, furniture conservation intern 1984-1986*)

Carol Warner (*National Museum Act intern 1979-1980*)

Marc Williams (*furniture conservation intern 1978*)

Gillian Wohlauer (*office assistant 1971-1972*)

David Wood (*department assistant 1985, National Museum Act intern 1984*)

Luis Neri Zagal (*assistant furniture restorer 1975-1976*)

Catherine Zusy (*research assistant 1985-1987*)

*deceased

Tom Loeser
(b. 1956)

113.
Chest (front and back cover)
Cambridge, Massachusetts, 1988
Cherry, curly maple, birch plywood; milk
paint
H. 20⅛ in., W. 59 in., D. 16 in.
Gift of the Seminarians and Anonymous Gift
1988.332

The Museum of Fine Arts has developed an extraordinary collection of contemporary American studio furniture. Beginning with the acquisition of twelve works by Sam Maloof in 1976 as part of the "Please Be Seated" program of gallery seating, the Department of American Decorative Arts and Sculpture has been a leader in recognizing the artistic talent of living furnituremakers. The department organized the important "New American Furniture" exhibition of 1989 to bring critical attention to the importance of such work.

Tom Loeser has been one of the leading studio furnituremakers in the use of paint as a compositional and decorative element. His recent work uses painted surfaces and naturally finished woods to provide a rich surface that bestows a deep emotive power to his objects. His designs demonstrate close study and understanding of the principles of historic furniture, but Loeser interprets such ideas in a fresh, innovative manner. Inspired by the simple joinery and carved corners of seventeenth-century board chests, Loeser used frame-and-panel construction for the front and back of this chest, but eschewed joints with flush planes, preferring instead to carry planes past each other and exaggerating this continuation with carved and painted saw-tooth edges. He made these edges with a backsaw and chisel rather than with a table saw jig. The work is time-consuming and requires considerable skill, but he has used this free workmanship to create a form of natural simplicity with painted decoration.
ESC

Credits:

Copyright© 1991 by the Museum of Fine Arts, Boston, Massachusetts

Library of Congress Catalogue Card No. 90-50834

ISBN 0-87846-332-1

Printed and typeset by Acme Printing Co., Wilmington, Massachusetts

Designed by Cynthia Rockwell Randall

Dates of the exhibition: January 10-April 14, 1991

Funded through generous contributions made by special friends and associates of the Department of American Decorative Arts and Sculpture.